Organizational Design

Organizational Design

Jeffrey Pfeffer

University of California, Berkeley

AHM Publishing Corporation
Arlington Heights, Illinois 60004

iv

Copyright © 1978

AHM PUBLISHING CORPORATION
All rights reserved

ISBN: 0-88295-453-9

Library of Congress Card Number: 77-86024

PRINTED IN THE UNITED STATES OF AMERICA
Second Printing
7108

Contents

Foreword

The growing awareness of the importance of organizations in our lives has created interest in understanding them. We are interested in individual and interpersonal behavior in organizations. We are aware that organizations influence us and that through our participation we can change organizations. We realize that organizations have subgroups, structures, and task and administrative processes. We understand that organizations are affected by technology, other organizations, and by general social and economic conditions. We also perceive that organizations can be used by their members in order to achieve personal goals.

Given the wide range of problems and issues, there are many theoretical approaches, schools of thought, and very different methods for studying organizational phenomena. This diversity has resulted in a growing, vigorous, and exciting field of study. It has also given rise

to a wide variety of academic courses and research interests.

The books in this series are more than a collection of separate surveys. They have been
integrated to provide a clear picture of the
scope of organizational behavior, to insure
consistency in approach, and to portray coher-
ently the relationships existing across sub-
problem areas. Each book cross references the
others, and together they provide an up-to-
date working library for any person seeking to
understand the field of organizational behavior.

To achieve these goals of integration and
completeness, six outstanding scholars and
teachers with experience teaching in business
schools were assembled to write the first six
books in this project. Two are social psycholo-
gists, three are specialists in organizational
behavior, and one is a sociologist. The wide
range of topics was first drawn up and then
divided into six groups. Each of the authors
then worked with the series editor to draw up
a detailed outline for his or her portion of
the whole work. Care was taken to insure that
each author understood how he or she related
to the whole series, that each author had a
theme for each chapter, and that these themes were
consistent within individual books and across
the series as a whole. When the independent
writing of each book was completed, the author
and the series editor went over each manuscript
painstakingly to create a solid part that was
consistent with the whole series. One of the
features of this series is that each book examines its topics in terms of behavioral processes. Behavior is seen in terms of complex
interrelated sequences of contingent events.

Each book is written so that it can stand
alone and so that it connects across the others
in the series. Thus, any single book or any
combination of books can be used in the class-
room. In addition to the coherence of an integrated series, the integration itself helped
to reduce the length of each book and hence reduce the direct costs to the student. The author

of each book had the primary responsibility of
writing on his or her assigned topics. But
when a topic from another book was needed, the
author could count on its being adequately
covered. Thus, each author could stick to specific topics and refer to the other books for
more detailed explanations for other topics.
Together these books provide adequate coverage
of the main topics, a compendium of ideas about
organizational behavior, and a source of new
ideas and critical references.

   The books in the series were written primarily for beginning M.B.A. students at a respect-
able college or university. Some of these
schools require two semesters or three quarters
of classes in organizational behavior. For
these, we recommend that all six books be used.
Some require a semester of classes. For these
we recommend any three of the books. Those requiring one or two quarters should use two or
four of these books.

Kenneth D. Mackenzie
Lawrence, 1977

Preface

Organizational design is currently a major topic in both the descriptive literature on formal organizations and the literature dealing with how to manage such organizations. The structural approach, if not replacing the emphasis on psychological concepts, has certainly gained importance in the literature of management and organizational behavior. It is well recognized that structures affect and constrain behavior, and affect performance, coordination, and the activities that go on in organizations. The importance of organizational structures has led to a spate of studies and books dealing with the analysis of structures and prescriptions concerning the use of the knowledge of organizational structure in designing organizations.

Given the tremendous literature on organizational design and organizational structure developed by the Aston group, by Blau and his students and colleagues, and by others operating

in this tradition, one might ask why another
book on organizational design is needed. I
think there are two answers to this question.
First, as a sociologist by inclination, I believe
in the importance of structure as a concept for
teaching about organizations. However, the
critical importance of design is not captured
in the current literature, at least in a way
that is meaningful to students. Second, there
is great interest in the political economy
perspective as a tool for organizational analysis. This tradition, emerging from the con-
ceptualizations of Cyert and March, and March
and Simon, emphasizes the importance of power
and conflict within organizations. Although
there have been a few empirical studies of
power and dependence, I am interested in seeing
whether this coalitional perspective can be
applied to structural issues as well. Such a
perspective would involve a shift in emphasis
and orientation, and it seems desirable to see
where such a theoretical formulation might
lead. There is a growing dissatisfaction with
the available literature on organizational
structure and design. Therefore, it seems useful to introduce another framework for analysis
to reorient and rejuvenate this body of inquiry.

There are two prominent divisions in the
literature on design. The first body of literature proceeds from large-scale, occasionally
longitudinal studies on various dimensions of
organizations and the relationships of these
dimensions to each other and to technology,
size, and organizational environments. This
literature, while large and rapidly expanding,
has some serious deficiencies. It is occasionally atheoretical. The development of elaborate
scales to measure hypothetical constructs,
factor analyzing the measures, and performing
other sophisticated quantitative analyses do
not constitute the development of a theory of
organizational structure. The lack of theory
has been commented on by others, such as Howard
Aldrich (1972). Whether size causes structure,
technology causes structure, or environment

causes structure, a sound theory accounting
for various predicted causal linkages is needed. As many others have noted, a path diagram
is not a theory. This first body of literature,
then, tends to be atheoretical. Moreover,
this literature is filled with a lot of terminology that is difficult for students (and,
I suspect a few professors) to decipher. The
sophistication of the data analyses has exceeded the sophistication of the questions
being asked.

The second body of literature on design is
more applied, more managerial, and much easier
to read. The best example of this genre is Jay
Galbraith's book (1973). Rather than relating
abstract concepts to each other, Galbraith sets
out to expose the reader to some considerations
and possible solutions to organizational coordination problems. Mechanisms for managing
large numbers of people doing a variety of
tasks that need to be coordinated are explored
in a systematic fashion in the work of the
Lawrence and Lorsch (1967) tradition.

Such an approach is quite seductive. It is
applied, clearly written, and based on reasonable theoretical foundations. But, as one con-
siders organizational life, it becomes clear
that issues such as efficiency, effectiveness,
and profit do not dominate all decisions and
activities. There is concern with getting
ahead, with getting one's way in the organization, with obtaining power and influence. The
problem with the second body of literature is
that it assumes an organizational goal, and
assumes this goal from the managerial point of
view. Now, this is fine for legitimating and
justifying managerial action, but such a perspective risks missing much of what is actually
going on in organizations, including in their
design.

The problem of goal orientation is present
in virtually all the literature on structure.
Although Thompson (1967) explicitly used the
concept of administrative rationality as the
basis for developing his propositions, adminis-

trative rationality in the Weberian sense underlies most of the work on organizational structures. Implicit in the hypotheses is the idea that structures are designed to control behavior in such a way as to produce efficient or effective organizational operation. Size, for instance, has its hypothesized effects on structure because size affects the need for co-ordination and the possibility of achieving economies of scale within the coordinating or administrating components. Both the need for coordination and the economy of scale conditions imply a concern with organizational efficiency and organizational performance. This goal of the organization is implied, and the task of structural analysis is to determine how best to design an organization to achieve the goal.

This book develops an alternative approach to analyzing and designing organizational structures. Viewing organizations as coalitions with ill-defined and inconsistent preferences, the perspective used here examines the relationship between issues of design and issues of organizational governance. We would assert that the central question to be asked in organizations is not how well are we doing, but to whom and for whom are we doing it? Governance, control, and political processes in organizations are related to issues of structure. This book presents an initial attempt to explore where such issues can lead in analyzing organizational design.

In chapter 1 we set the tone for the book, raising the fundamental issue of who governs, and detailing our conceptual model of organizations and decision making. Design appears to be both an outcome and a cause of power and influence in organizations, and the determinants of power, and how organizational political systems might be unobtrusively assessed, are detailed. We also define organizational design, and then note that the issue of governance includes control by parties generally considered to be outside of the organization's boundaries.

In chapter 2 the dimensions of design are described and related to the task of managing interdependence among people. The next three chapters describe three variables that affect the control and governance process, and consequently design. In chapter 3 we discuss management information and evaluation systems, in chapter 4 technology, and in chapter 5, the environment. In each instance an attempt is made to relate research and theorizing to the question of who governs and the related question of the distribution of influence within organizations. We consider technology and information systems to be strategic variables that both affect but are also affected by the contest for control.

Chapter 6 pursues the strategic orientation as we consider ways organizations seek to control or manage their environments. Design of external systems of interdependence may be as critical, if not more so, than designing internal structures. Change and how structures evolve are the topics of chapter 7. In chapter 8 we consider in some detail the design of a university as a case illustration of some of the concepts. Chapter 9 serves both to summarize the argument and to illustrate its application in exploring some additional issues currently topical in the field of design, such as participative management and power equalization, differentiation, and consumer affairs departments.

The goal of this book is simple—to argue for a new approach to understanding organizations and their design that does not adopt without thinking a managerialist, rationalist perspective on organizational analysis. It is my hope that readers of this book will be sensitized to the issues of control, influence, and power that will profoundly affect them, their careers, and the organizations in which they will work. Few people are ever in a position to design whole organizations. All of us are in a position in which it is helpful to be able to predict what designs are likely to be, and why, and how we can successfully use our resources.

Ken Mackenzie, who offered me the opportunity to write this book, has my thanks. Our association goes back several years, and he has always provided me with provocative ideas and helpful criticism.

One other person deserves special mention— Susan M. Pfeffer. Anyone who has seen the University of California salary schedules can realize that I am able to do things like teach, research, and write books only because I have outside support, graciously and unselfishly provided. Without Susan I might have to sell real estate, sweep streets, or do something else to increase my income and permit us to live in the style to which we have become accustomed. Her support during the writing of this book made it all possible.

REFERENCES

Aldrich, Howard E. "Technology and Organizational Structure: A Reexamination of the Findings of the Aston Group." *Administrative Science Quarterly 17* (1972): 26–43.

Galbraith, Jay. *Designing Complex Organizations*. Reading, Mass.: Addison-Wesley, 1973.

Lawrence, Paul, and Lorsch, Jay. *Organization and Environment*. Boston, Mass.: Division of Research, Harvard Business School, 1967.

Thompson, James D. *Organizations in Action*. New York: McGraw-Hill, 1967.

1

Who Governs?

There are two analytical questions that can be asked of any social group: (1) how resources, legitimacy, and effort are organized and directed to produce collective benefits or output; and (2) how the benefits, these outputs of the collective effort, are distributed. Gamson (1968) posed these two alternative questions as complementary perspectives for analyzing social power and influence. Each asks about a different aspect of organizations. One asks about how organizations are structured, managed, and controlled to produce goods or services. The second asks who gets what, when, and how (Lasswell, 1935) from the organization—who decides what to produce, and who gets the benefits of the collective effort. The issues are intertwined. The mobilization of collective effort is related to the issue of who benefits and how much from the effort.

Traditional approaches to organizational design have emphasized the creation-of-output

problem. Studies focus on determining optimal
organizational designs for various technological and environmental contingencies—optimal in
the sense of being either: (a) more profitable,
or (b) more productive. The fact that the goods
or services should be produced at all—the organizational goal, if you will—is taken as
given. The assumption of productivity or profit
as the overriding concern implicitly takes the
point of view of the ownership or managerial
interests of the organization.

From this perspective, organizational design
is like an engineering problem (Child, 1973).
Organizational structure, the relationships
among positions in the organization, is something to be adjusted, turned, or twisted until
better results occur. Organizational design is
a tool in the manager's tool kit, and the manager is presumed to be interested in effectiveness, profit, or outputs. A representative
definition of organizational design is this:
"Design is essentially the activity of con-
structing and changing organizational structure
to achieve optimum effectiveness" (Calder,
Rowland, and Leblebici, 1974, p. 1).

This view of organizational design takes the
production of a collective output as the critical problem. Structures should be designed to
maximize the organization's productivity. Thus,
Miles has written, "The prime implication is
that management must design a structure which,
in contrast to the traditional hierarchy, is
aimed more at facilitating positive contributions than at controlling deviant performance"
(1975, p. 84). But Gamson (1968) noted that the
problem of the authorities was control of behavior, and control is a central theme in much
of the literature on bureaucracies and organizations. From Weber (1947) to Ouchi and Dowling
(1974), the control of behavior in organizations has been viewed as an objective of organizational rules, systems of evaluation, and
structure. The conflict between control of behavior and presumed individual needs has been
commented on by Argyris (1957), and the

techniques of control are prominent in the
social, psychological, and sociological literature on organizations—socialization, social
influence, conformity, social learning, and
role behavior.

But the issue is not, as implied by Miles'
comment quoted above, that the strategies of
management are inappropriate. It is possible
that control itself, not control as a means of
ensuring the efficient production of output,
becomes the objective of action. When there is
conflict over goals and technology, the control
of the organization is the problem confronted
by the authorities. It is the theme of this
book that the problems of organizational design
are concerned with control, not merely with the
best way to produce more output.

GOVERNANCE AND ORGANIZATIONAL CHOICE

While organizational theorists may not, other
persons understand quite clearly the central
importance of the question of who governs. On
the tenth anniversary of the Free Speech Movement,[1] an editorial under the title "Who
Governs?" appeared in the Berkeley student
newspaper.

> But another cause also motivated the Free Speechers—
> the question of who rightfully governs the University.
> A central issue in the Free Speech Movement was wheth-
> er the aloof and historically conservative Board of
> Regents could unilaterally direct the affairs of the
> University, unmoved by the desires and opinions of
> those who attended, taught for, or worked for the
> institution (The *Daily Californian*, October 2, 1974,
> p. 5).

Many of the issues negotiated in labor-man-
agement disputes involve the question of who
has the right to dictate the terms and conditions of employment and the conduct of workers
on the job. In other words, the issues again
frequently revolve around who controls, and
what is the scope and operation of the control.

At the opening of the 94th Congress there was
a contest for the control of committee chair-
manships, with the basis for allocation and the
outcomes of this process being questioned by
the less senior members, particularly in the
House of Representatives. Consumers also have
made claims for increased control over the
activities of business organizations, demanding
more say as to what the corporation's policies,
products, and prices are. Indeed, it is difficult to think of any organization in which the
issue of control is not problematic, and in
which there are not contesting groups contending for control over the allocation and use of
the organization's resources.

Our theme is simple. Organizations make
choices, and the bases for these organizational
decisions—who makes them and why—is an important analytical question to be asked about organizations. Since organizations are frequently
large, and our society is, indeed, dominated by
organizations (Boulding, 1953), the choices
and decisions made by organizations are important. These decisions are important because of
their effect on our lives as individuals working in or being served by organizations, and
because of their effect on how society's resources are allocated and used.

The next logical question is, then, who benefits and who controls these organizations. It
is only reasonable to assume that organizational benefits are not equally distributed.
The question of control and governance becomes
important in affecting what organizations do,
and who benefits. Decisions must be made on the
allocation of organizational resources. It is
unreasonable to assume that people are disin-
terested observers of this process. Rather, organizational participants are in a contest for
resources and their control. This contest is
political and is fought in many contexts within
organizations. One context is the structural
arrangement of positions and persons within organizations. Design is an important factor affecting who controls organizations, who governs.

Since there is a contest for control, there is
a contest and conflict over organizational design. Organizational structure is, indeed, an
important factor in organizational control, but
control and design are the outcomes of power
and influence operating within organizations.

A View of Organizations

It is appropriate to make explicit the con-
ceptualization of organizations behind our discussion. There are two prominent perspectives
on organizations. One sees organizations as
having goals, and the problem of management is
to recruit, train, control, and motivate organizational participants so as to achieve the
organization's goal (or goals). This is the
virtually universal perspective adopted in the
management literature on organizations. The
second view of organizations sees them as coalitions, composed of varying groups and individuals with different demands. Cyert and
March (1963) developed this perspective in
their critique of conventional economic treatments of the theory of the firm (see March,
1962). A coalition model of organizations posits that coalition participants must receive
inducements from belonging greater than the
contributions they are required to make. Coalition members, then, are continually calculating
whether to remain in the organization, or
whether they might fare better if they altered
their participation. In addition to the allocation of resources, policies and policy commitments are important, and they are the objects
of bargaining as well.

Since the organization is viewed as a coalition of many participants, the organization's
goal becomes a concept with little meaning. As
Cyert and March (1963, p.30) pointed out, it
makes as much sense to talk of the organization's goal as maximizing the janitor's salary
as it does maximizing profits. Owners and jani-
tors are both coalition participants. If either

does not receive enough from coalition membership, withdrawal is likely. But speaking of the organization's goal as being the goal of the owners assumes a degree of control and acceptance of this control by other organizational participants that probably is infrequent.

The coalition view of organizations strongly implies that there will be conflict over objectives, rather than consensus over one or a few organizational goals. Since the organization is composed of persons with varying backgrounds and perspectives, occupying varying positions, it is only natural that differences in criteria for evaluating organizational actions develop. The shop floor worker, the personnel manager, the principal stockholder, and the foreman are not likely to have the same objectives or criteria for evaluating the organization's operations.

There is empirical evidence supporting the view that organizations serve many interests with conflicting criteria. Friedlander and Pickle (1968) examined the effectiveness of 96 small businesses in Texas, asking about organizational effectiveness from the perspectives of the owners, employees, creditors, suppliers, customers, and local and federal governments. The authors found that there were either small or slightly negative correlations among the assessments of how well an organization satisfied each of these seven groups. The authors concluded that organizations served many interests, and moreover, could not simultaneously please all of them equally well.

There are also likely to be disagreements concerning the connections between actions and outcomes. Organizational technology is frequently as uncertain as organizational goals. A recent example illustrates what we mean. Early in 1975, there was general agreement on the goal of reducing energy use, and particularly gasoline consumption, in the United States. But differences of opinion existed concerning the connections between actions and

results. Some believed that raising the price
would restrict consumption, though there was
uncertainty about how much reduction would be
achieved for how much price increase (the
elasticity of demand was unknown). Other effects were equally in dispute. Similarly, in
organizations there may be agreement over the
goal, perhaps to maximize profits, but there
may be disagreements concerning strategies or
actions to achieve these goals.

One source of disagreement is that different
participants in the organization have access to
different information. The information that a
marketing manager has, and the data possessed
by the production manager, are fundamentally
different. Data differences may lead to differences in the interpretation of problems, as
well as to differences in beliefs about solutions. Secondly, there are differences in
training and socialization which orient managers to attend to different aspects of the situation, and to look to different strategies for
solution. Dearborn and Simon (1958) illustrated
this phenomenon nicely in a study conducted on
business executives attending a training ses-
sion. A business case was given to the executives, and the problem in the case was identified as a finance problem by the finance executives, a marketing problem by the marketing
executives, a production problem by the production executives. Differences in background,
socialization, training, and information all
may cause differences in beliefs about the
likely outcomes of organizational actions. Ad-
ditionally, there may simply be not enough information to assess the connections between actions and results. Frequently, organizations
confront novel situations and, lacking experience, are uncertain about the effectiveness of
alternative decisions.

WHERE'S RATIONALITY?

Much of the organization and management literature is prescriptive in tone, and one of the

criteria for evaluating decision-making that is
frequently proposed is that of rationality.
Rationality is linked to the process of choice
(Friedland, 1974), and is generally construed
to mean choosing that course of action which
will maximize the chooser's expected utility.
The concept of utility recognizes that outcomes may have different values to different
persons, and the concept of expectation recognizes that decisions may be made under conditions of uncertainty. However, what this concept of rationality does not address is how to
cope with conflicting standards of assessment,
the fact that goals may not be shared among the
organizational participants. Arrow (1951)
showed that there is no general method of ag-
gregating the ordinal preferences of individuals into a single ordered pattern of social
preferences consistent with a number of assumptions used to describe rationality.

Simply put, since rationality is defined with
respect to some preference for outcomes, when
there is no consensus on outcome preferences
it is difficult to speak of rationality.
Thompson and Tuden (1959) have developed a useful typology of decision-making structures and
situations. They wrote that when there is
agreement on goals and on the beliefs about the
connections between actions and results, a
computational mode of decision-making could be
employed. But when disagreements arose, some
other form of decision-making, using judgment
or compromise, was required. The computational
mode of decision-making corresponds to the
definitions of rationality, indicating that
rationality is defined and achieved only in
those instances where there is agreement over
objectives and technology.

Thus, one problem in speaking of the rationality of organizational actions is caused by
attributing a goal to an essentially diverse
coalition of interests. Another difficulty with
the concept of rational choice is a challenge
posed to the concept of a goal at even the individual level of analysis. Weick (1969),

following Schutz (1967), has argued that the
meaning of action is inferred retrospectively,
or after the action has occurred. In this
formulation, goals and other attitude statements are attempts to make sense out of actions
that have already occurred, rather than plans
for the future. The similarity between this
perspective and some elements of attribution
theory (Kelley, 1971) should be apparent. In
both cases, the argument is that meaning is
inferred by the observer from the action, and
since the action must have occurred in order
for it to be examined, then meaning in both
instances is inferred retrospectively.

The possibility that behavior is not goal-
directed is one that is difficult for most
people to accept. Yet all of us can think of
everyday experiences in which we were able,
after the fact, to explain—rationalize—our
actions much better than we could before we
engaged in them; similarly with planning. When
I ask my students to develop a career plan,
they have a great deal of difficulty, not only
because of uncertainty concerning future
events, but also because they cannot foresee
how their preferences will change through experience. Conversely, they are very good at
explaining their past behavior. Past action is
real; the future is less concrete. It is not
illogical, then, to expect the reality of our
past behavior to have a major influence in
shaping statements of our goals and opinions.
We are assimilators of past experience, and
meaning is at least partly inferred from retro-
spective examinations of our behavior.

Two Examples

Two examples illustrate how difficult it is
to talk of rationality in real organizational
decision-making situations. One is the construction of the Bay Area Rapid Transit System
(BART). This is a well-publicized major effort
to construct a new, modern, efficient transportation system for the San Francisco Bay

Area. More complete histories of this system
can be found in Homburger (1967) and Wolfe
(1968). For the present, it is sufficient to
note the following: (1) the initial planning
committees instrumental in planning for BART
were dominated by companies that stood to benefit either directly from the work of the project or indirectly through their positions in
real estate or their possible involvement as
underwriters of the BART financing; (2) the appointed board of directors was generally un-
familiar with the engineering and technical aspects of the project; (3) the largest donors to
the Citizens for Rapid Transit, the group that
advertised in favor of the special bond elec-
tion to finance BART in 1962, were the Bank of
America, Wells Fargo, Crocker Bank, Tudor
Engineering, Bechtel, Westinghouse Electric,
Bethlehem Steel, Kaiser Industries, Perini
Corporation (real estate), Westinghouse Air
Brake, the Downtown Property Owner's Association, and Parsons, Brinckerhoff, Quade, and
Douglas (engineering consulting) (Wolfe, 1968);
(4) Parsons, in a joint venture with Tudor and
Bechtel, was retained as the engineering consultant for system design and construction,
with an open-ended fee arrangement which
climbed from its initially expected $47 million
to over $120 million; (5) BART was completed
years late, at a cost of $1.6 billion rather
than the originally estimated figure of about
$900 million.

Our question is: Was this a rational organizational process, effective in serving its intended goals? It should be obvious that the
answer to this question is very much dependent
on where in the coalition one is. From the
perspective of a taxpayer, burdened with both
a special sales tax increment and property
tax increments as well, many aspects of the
system were not rational or effective. From
the perspective of the contributors to Citizens for Rapid Transit, all of whom have
enriched themselves enormously from the
contracts involved in the construction, the

project was both successful and rational. Indeed, the higher the costs and the greater the difficulties, the better for Bechtel and its joint venture associates, which could make fees designing the system, and would make additional fees fixing it when it did not work. The moral: What looks like irrational behavior, leading to inefficiency, is only irrational to those not profiting from the extra revenues generated.

Our second example involves the allocation of faculty positions to subject area groups within, say, a school of business. Further, let us assume that class enrollments are the only factor to be considered. Here, you might expect, is a computational decision situation if there ever were one. After all, a student is a student, and we can all count students and faculty. But, does an undergraduate student count the same as an M.B.A., or an M.B.A. the same as an advanced M.B.A. taking an elective, or a Ph.D. student? Is a course taught by an instructor the same as one taught by an assistant professor, or one by a full professor? And, how about students who take the courses from other departments? How should they be weighted in determining resource needs by the various subject areas? It is probably the case that in any real situation, the resource-allocation implications are altered greatly, depending upon how these weights are assigned. And while it is true that there are facts—the number of students of what types, and the composition of the faculty—it is far from a computational procedure to determine how varying students should be counted for purposes of allocating resources, although once the weightings are assigned, the actual decision-making appears to be routine. Here is an instance in which there is ostensible agreement on the criterion, allocating positions based on teaching loads, and there is plenty of objective data, and even so, the possibility remains of conflict and influence being associated with the decision.

It is difficult to think of situations in

which goals are so congruent, or the facts so clear-cut that judgment and compromise are not involved. What is rational from one point of view is irrational from another. Organizations are political systems, coalitions of interests, and rationality is defined only with respect to unitary and consistent orderings of preferences.

A Model of Organizational Choice

That decisions are not made computationally or bureaucratically, that goals are hard to identify, does not mean that decisions are made in a random fashion. Rather, when consensually agreed upon, objective standards are missing from the situation, social power and influence affect the outcome of decisions. This statement is well supported by the literature from social psychology. Festinger (1954) noted that persons sought social referents for their beliefs and attitudes. Smith (1973) noted that ambiguity, because of this need for the social anchoring of beliefs, could lead to situations of informational social influence— social influence that derives from the reduction of uncertainty, not from hierarchical position or the possession of money or other inducements. In an ambiguous, uncertain situation, social influence is likely to operate to influence the decision's outcome.

Social power and influence are also more likely to operate when the resource being allocated is scarce or the decision being made is important (Salancik and Pfeffer, 1974). There is no point contending when the decision is not critical. And there is not a decision problem or a problem of allocation unless there is some element of scarcity. If every person can get all he wants, or what he wants, then there is no need to use social power and influence, because everyone can be satisfied simultaneously.

Finally, social power and influence can operate when decision processes are more hidden from public scrutiny. Most people instinctively sense this, wanting to know the criteria by which they are being evaluated, how these criteria are measured, and how they are combined. We distrust decision-making done in secret, suspecting that the process may not be equitable, particularly for those who are not participants.

Goal statements and objective criteria are used in the decision-making process as arguing points, and are used selectively depending on who benefits from their application. In interviews with 29 department heads at the University of Illinois, Salancik and Pfeffer (1974) reported that each head tended to favor basing budget allocations on criteria which tended to favor his own department. These authors concluded that power was used to affect the criteria for decisions. This is a reasonable position, since it is unlikely that in a meeting to make a decision a person will say, "Give more to my subunit because we are more powerful." Rather, social influence will be used to affect the goals or criteria so as to favor that subunit.

This view of organizational choice suggests that influence within the organization is an important factor in explaining variance in the decisions made. There is some empirical support for this position. Stagner (1969), in a survey of business executives, reported that the executives said that strong subunits within the organization were frequently able to get their way without regard for the welfare of the whole organization. And Pfeffer and Salancik (1974), examining budget allocations to departments in a university, reported that even after controlling for objective factors, social influence accounted for a significant amount of the variation in resource allocation. When computational modes of decision-making are impossible because of conflict over goals or uncertainty concerning technology, the power of participants in the coalition comes to affect the decisions made.

The coalitional model of organizations seems

to imply a continual contest for power and a
continual process of conflict and negotiation.
Such an outcome is only partially observed.
Individuals enter and leave the contest as
their strength and interests dictate, but some
level of change and negotiation does continue
as a process in the organization. Conflict is
uncomfortable to most organizational participants, and moreover, to undertake long strug-
gles over each decision would be too time-
consuming. Consequently, precedent becomes
very important in organizational decision-making. Once an acceptable basis for resource allocation is achieved or once a set of policies
is adopted, precedent becomes the guide to
future organizational decisions. This avoids
reopening negotiations, which might reactivate
the conflict and involve a lot of time and effort. Davis, Dempster, and Wildavsky (1966)
noted that the best predictors of a U.S. government agency's current budget are its budget
last year, its request for the current year,
and factors that represent its growth and ability to obtain incremental budget from Congress.
Incrementalism saves analytical effort and
recognizes the cognitive and information-processing limitations of both persons and organizations. Incrementalism and precedent will
operate as long as the existing balance of influence remains relatively stable. When, however, the distribution of influence within the
organization shifts dramatically from what it
had been when the initial set of bargains was
reached, it is likely that those who have
gained influence will attempt to reopen the
negotiation, seeking to throw away precedent
and to establish a new basis for future organizational actions.

Since there are fundamental disagreements
over criteria, goals, and even the definition
of the situation, control of the organization
becomes an important issue. If there were
agreement over objectives and technology, then
control would be unimportant, because the decisions and policies would be identical, no

matter who was in power. Because of the disagreements and uncertainty, control is critical in determining organizational actions.

Because of disagreements over goals, and because of the differences in backgrounds and information possessed by organizational participants, organizational decisions are affected by the location in the organization where they are made and where the problem is located. Cyert and March (1963) made this argument when they noted that the search for solutions tends to begin in a localized fashion, starting first by focusing on that part of the organization in which the problem was first noticed. So, if a company is losing its share of the market, if the problem is identified first by and in the marketing department, it will probably initially be viewed as a marketing problem. The advertising budget and strategy will be examined, and the organization and effectiveness of the sales force will be analyzed. Only later will the search be extended to examine other sources of the problem, such as delays in delivery caused by production, or by the inability to give competitive credit terms as a result of policies set in the finance department. The fact of localized search makes the organization's information-gathering and transmission structure very important in determining organizational actions. If problem definition determines the likely initial course of behavior, then where and by whom the problem is located accounts for much of the variance in possible responses.

DETERMINANTS OF SOCIAL POWER

We have argued that because of the coalitional nature of organizations, few decisions are made computationally, and most decisions are affected by subunit and individual power within the organization. The answer to the question of who controls or governs the organization is that person or group with the most power. It is

relevant to our consideration of organizational
design as an outcome and as a factor in the
contest for control that dimensions of organizational structure have a great deal to do with
the distribution and possession of power in organizations.

FORMAL AUTHORITY

There are few people who are not familiar
with an organization chart, that formal representation of positions and their relationship
to one another within the organization. Although we also know about informal organizations, and the fact that the chart does not
tell everything about the organization's functioning, the formal structure of an organization does provide one determinant of power and
control. Coupled with job descriptions delimiting responsibilities, the formal structure
specifies who reports to whom and who has the
authority to evaluate another person. The
evaluation process is central in the process of
controlling behavior within organizations
(Scott, et al., 1967). These authority rights
are conveyed through the formal hierarchy—it
is typically, though not inevitably, the case
that a person in a given level has the right
to evaluate those persons who are immediately
below him and linked to him in the hierarchy
(see Simmons, 1978).

When a person goes to work, he implicitly
enters into an agreement that involves receiving pay and other benefits in return for
giving some control over his behavior to the
organization, and more specifically, his designated supervisor. We make these bargains so
often, trading money for our freedom of action
on the job, that we seldom think about them.
Nevertheless, the first and frequently the most
important determinant of governance is the
formal hierarchy of evaluation and authority
existing in the organization.

CONTROL OVER RESOURCES

Yet another basis for power in an organization is the possession of control over critical resources. Salancik and Pfeffer (1974)
found that the best predictor of department
power in a university was the amount of outside
money the department brought in. Pfeffer and
Leong (1977) examined the allocations of United
Funds to member agencies in a number of cities,
and found again that the ability to raise outside support was a principal determinant of
power within the coalition. Organizations require resources for survival. Control over
resources critical to the organization provides
a person or subunit with power in the organization.

Control over resources is affected by the
division of labor in the organization and
one's position in the resultant social structure. For example, consider possible alternative methods of allocating university-funded
scholarships. Under one system, suppose we
create an Office of Scholarships and Financial
Aid, and place in charge of that office a
director with the responsibility of allocating
scholarships to the individual departments.
Alternatively, suppose we have a similarly
titled office, but in this instance, the director is merely responsible for raising funds;
allocations to the departments are based solely
on the number of students enrolled. It is clear
that, other things being equal, in the former
case the occupant of the position of Director
of Scholarships and Financial Aid will have
more power in the organization. Similar examples readily come to mind for other organizational settings—job descriptions and the allocations of task leave the control of resources differentially distributed in the organization. Power and control accrue to those
positions with the most discretionary control
over critical and scarce resources.

INFORMATION AND ACCESS

One special resource is information, and access to and control of channels of communication. This resource is different enough from
financial resources, however, to bear special
discussion. One's position in the organizational structure profoundly affects the amount
of information one possesses, and one's centrality in the communication network. Both of
these factors, information and communication
centrality, profoundly affect the ability of
the position's occupant to wield power in the
organization.

Once again, we shall provide some examples.
Power can accrue to a person because of his
position in the flow of communication, and
therefore because of his ability to filter,
summarize, and analyze information as it is
passed. In one university, the head of a department resigned, and a search was instituted
for a replacement. The department was a subunit in a college, and the college had an executive committee that advised the Dean. The ap-
pointment was the responsibility of the Dean.
As is occasionally done, the Dean appointed a
search committee to locate qualified candidates. The search committee was to report its
recommendations to the executive committee,
and through it, to the Dean. It so happened
that one inside candidate for the job was appointed to the search committee, and was also
on the college executive committee. Initially,
this candidate had little support in either
the search committee or the executive committee; however, as the months wore on, he emerged
as the leading contender. This was accomplished
by systematically providing information between
the two committees that led to the elimination
of our candidate's principal competitors from
consideration. Since he was the only person
serving on both committees, he reported between the two, and in the process served his
own interests.

The importance of access gives power to many staff positions (Tuggle, 1978). The ability to buffer, filter, and selectively provide information enables one to control the information and even the premises on which decisions will be made. Access to and control of information comes from one's position in the social structure.

And then we have the case of using information to centralize control. Currently, many universities face financial difficulty. In times of resource scarcity, the argument goes, decisions concerning the use of resources must be made as carefully and as effectively as possible. In order to accomplish this, elaborate evaluation and information-gathering systems have been established on many university campuses, involving the expansion in both numbers and functions of the data-processing units. In the University of California system and on the campus level, such positions report directly to administrative officers of the highest level. The implications of all of this for control are evident by attending any meeting. While the faculty have opinions, values, beliefs, and eloquence, the vice chancellor (or the chancellor, or the president) has the computer output. "The facts" usually win, as many students have learned when they use elaborate presentations in case preparations to "snow" the instructor or the class. By controlling information, one controls the premises of the discussion and the outcome.

It is, therefore, not surprising that some of the most bitter fights have occurred in organizations over the placement or movement of the computer or information-processing department. Managers instinctively know that control of the information system is tantamount to control over the organization, and the contest for this function is intense.

UNCERTAINTY REDUCTION

The most prominent current explanation for

power in organizations is the ability to cope with critical organizational uncertainty. Crozier (1964) illustrated this with his example of the maintenance engineers in a French plant. Because the breakdown of machinery was the only remaining contingency faced by the organization, the maintenance engineers came to have extraordinary influence, particularly because they had the foresight to keep their expertise in their heads rather than on paper where others could acquire it. Thompson (1967) based his discussion of power also on the ability to deal with uncertainty, and the capability of coping with uncertainty is the central variable in Hickson et al.'s (1971) strategic contingencies' theory of intraorganizational power. Hickson and his colleagues also argued that power was increased to the extent that uncertainty was pervasive or important in the organization, and to the extent that the coping capability could not be easily replaced.

We noted earlier in this chapter that theories of informal social communication also emphasize the importance of coping with uncertainty. Smith (1973) explained that in conditions of uncertainty, informational social influence is possible as people seek to resolve the uncertainty, and Festinger (1954) demonstrated that uncertainty leads to increased social communication. Uncertainty, then, provides the subunit or group that can reduce it with the opportunity to obtain increased control in the organization.

The ability to reduce organizational uncertainty again depends on the position in the social structure. Clearly, the capability of reducing uncertainty is related to one's access to information, the position in the communication structure, and also the possession of resources valued by the organization. More specifically, roles and tasks can be restructured to give certain positions either more or less influence in the organization. As Thompson (1967, p. 129) has written, decentralization creates more power positions, but lessens the organization's dependence on any single one. Subdividing a task into very simple components makes it easier to substitute employees, lessening the power of any single employee. The routinization of functions such as production scheduling, financial analysis or other managerial tasks diminishes the influence of those employees whose tasks have been made less uncertain.

I once was interviewed for a summer job at a large food-manufacturing facility. On this occasion, I spoke with the executive in charge of one product division. It so happened that in this division, production scheduling was done by a man in his 60s not using the most sophisticated methods of operations research, occasionally with disastrous results. Nevertheless, the attempt to hire bright, young M.B.A.'s to update the forecasting technology was singularly unsuccessful. This man, scheduling by intuition, practice, and experience, resisted any attempts either to routinize or otherwise to change his function that might reduce his influence in the organization. More than occasionally, resistance to organizational change originates from those whose jobs are being redefined in such a way as to diminish the uncertainty and discretion associated with them, and consequently, the influence of the job holders.

Assessing Power in Social Structures

If power is important in determining organizational choice, including the choice of structures, then it is critical for organizational participants to be able to diagnose systems of organizational influence. To contend in a political process, one must at least be able to diagnose the distribution of power and the preferences and demands of the other participants. There are several approaches to assessing the power of various organizational actors. One approach involves determining the sources of power in the system, and then assessing how much of each source each organizational actor (individual, actor, or subunit) possesses. This procedure is equivalent to Gamson's (1968) suggestion that since power derives from resources, one can assess power by assessing the resources controlled by various social actors. In the study of determinants of power in a university, Salancik and Pfeffer (1974) assessed how important various resources brought into the organization by subunits were to the total organization. One could then argue that those subunits that controlled or accounted for more critical resources would have the most power. If uncertainty reduction is important, then power should accrue to those subunits that can reduce the most critical uncertainty, and for which few substitutes are available. The first way of assessing power, then, is simply to determine what are sources of power, and see how much of these sources various participants possess.

Power is used in affecting organizational decisions and thus becomes visible. In addition to examining the sources of power, systems of influence can be diagnosed by examining the outcroppings of the effects of power in organizations. For instance, power may be used to affect the choice of organizational leaders, the distribution of scarce and critical resources, and the implementation of favored rules, policies, and procedures. Pfeffer and Salancik (1974) argued that representation on important committees might be both a source of power and a reflection of the existing structure of influence in universities. Their committee-based measures of power accounted for more of the variance in budget allocations than did interview-derived measures,though both measures were highly correlated. The affiliation of the chief executive officer and other officials in major executive positions and on important committees frequently provides information about the distribution of power. This is true in both corporations, universities, and

other organizations. If the chief executive in
a corporation always comes from marketing, or
if the dean of a business school is always an
economist, in both instances there is a clue
about power in the organization.

There are typically many possible outcroppings of the use of power, and the shrewd ana-
lyst will look for convergence in the measures,
since any single indicator may be affected by
random error or chance. In an assignment to
diagnose the distribution of influence among
subject areas in a school of business, an
M.B.A. class came up with a large number of
possible indicators, including the academic
affiliations of chief administrative officers,
the number of required courses in the various
subjects, the relative teaching loads and
student/faculty ratios, the representation on
important committees, the success in obtaining
promotions, and increments in total faculty
positions. Important committees tend to be
those associated with the allocation of resources, while unimportant committees can be
discovered by determining which are easy to get
on and which serve only ceremonial functions or
have relatively less powerful functions, such
as dealing with low-power clients.

The importance of using multiple measures
cannot be overemphasized. One should look for
convergence in indicators of subunit or personal power in making diagnoses of structures of
organizational influence. It also helps to assess power as unobtrusively as possible. Since
power is not a legitimate basis for organizational action, persons will likely be reluctant
to provide honest and accurate assessments of
power positions (see Pettigrew, 1973). Furthermore, asking about power may be perceived as
threatening, illegitimate, or excessively naive. Reports from colleagues or outside observers about distributions of power should
always be checked against the realities of the
determinants and outcomes of power. It is,
after all, in the interests of power holders to
hinder the accurate diagnosis of actual systems

of influence. Power is best exercised unobtrusively, and must, consequently, be diagnosed in a similar fashion.

WHAT IS ORGANIZATIONAL DESIGN?

We have talked in this chapter about one view
of organizations, and how this way of thinking
makes the issue of organizational control and
governance very important for understanding the
decisions and actions taken by organizations.
We have briefly explored some determinants of
power and influence in organizations, and have
sketched how organizational structure may be
related to these factors. It is now time to
describe explicitly what is meant by organizational design and organizational structure.

Structure has been defined as the patterning
of relationships or activities in organizations (Thompson, 1967, p. 51). As Weick (1969)
has noted, structure is a picture, at a given
time, of a continuing process of organizing.
This theme has been developed by Mackenzie
(1978) who describes the relationship between
process and structure. We can look at activities such as the use or nonuse of various half-
channels in a communication network to cope
with a particular task, and represent these
relationships in a structure. It is important
to remember that structure is nothing more than
the relationships among positions or roles in
an organization, and since relationships
change, structures change also.

Thompson (1967, ch. 5) argued that organizational structures developed in the following
way. Activities within organizations are differentiated—different people do different
parts of the task. Because the total task is
subdivided, the differentiated roles in the
organization are interdependent. Interdependence requires coordination. In the case of
designing an automobile, the size of the
engine and the size of the hood are interdependent. In the case of the Chevrolet Monza

2+2, when Chevrolet decided not to introduce
the rotary engine, but substitute a V-8 instead, someone forgot to take this into account
in designing the engine compartment. Thus,
Chevrolet produced a car in which, to change
one of the eight spark plugs, it was necessary
to unmount and partially lift the engine. Organizational structures are presumably developed to coordinate the interdependence among
activities in organizations, and Thompson
further hypothesized that structures would develop so as to minimize the costs of coordination and communication.

In this conception, organization design is
the process of grouping activities, roles, or
positions in the organization to coordinate effectively the interdependencies that exist. In
the literature on organizational design (e.g.,
Galbraith, (1973), the implicit goal of the
structuring process is achieving a more rationalized and coordinated system of activity.

As we have stated throughout this chapter, it
is not only tasks that are allocated and distributed throughout organizations. Control over
resources, legitimate authority, and control
of decision-making are also distributed. In
addition to talking of the relationship between
interdependent tasks, we can talk of the relationship between resource holders, between
persons with varying authority rights, and between positions with varying degrees of decision-making authority.

Structure is a continuing process of activity, but change is not as frequent as one might
expect. Weick (1969) cautioned that we should
focus on the incredible regularities in behavior in organizations, and not just on episodic instances of change. Patterns of behavior
are maintained by rules and procedures that may
be formally written down, or by informally but
strongly held norms about behavior. Mackenzie
(1978) has referred to these as behavioral con-
stitutions. Rules develop about changes in
structure, and about the allocation of tasks
and activities among group participants. These

rules and norms are reinforced by systems of
evaluation, frequently administered through
the formal hierarchy of authority. Everyone in
an organization is constantly evaluated, not
only by his organizational supervisor, but also
by his peers and his subordinates. Kahn et al.
(1964) describe the set of persons a given occupant of a position interacts with as that
person's role set. Everyone in the role set
has expectations for the focal person's behavior, and evaluates on a more or less frequent basis the extent to which his expectations are being met. Evaluation, and the subsequent administration of rewards and punishments, help to maintain the stability of relationships and activities in the organization.
    Structure involves relationships, including
authorizations to evaluate, the differential
distribution of the right to reward and punish,
the unequal allocation of information, resources, and the capability of coping with uncertainty, and as a consequence, differences in
power, influence, and control within organizations. Assuming conflicts over preferences and
goals, as well as over beliefs about the consequences of actions, structures become one
focus for the contest over control, and at a
given time, provide differential governance to
various organizational participants. There are,
it appears, two perspectives for analyzing
social structures. One asks the appropriateness
of a given structure for the coordination of
interdependence to achieve some task; the other
asks why and how structure is a result of organizational influence processes and the consequences of a given structure for the distribution of control and power within organizations. It is likely that these are complementary rather than competing perspectives. Because the usual emphasis is on the question of
designing structures for task achievement, this
book analyzes structure primarily from the
latter perspective of influence and control.

NOTES

[1]The Free Speech Movement was a precursor of much of the political action on college campuses and led to a great deal of turmoil at Berkeley. It originated over the issue of placing tables of literature and leaflets on Sproul Plaza, situated between an administration building and the student union complex. Such literature, and associated speeches and rallies in the plaza, were frequently political, and as such, embarrassing to the university. With the subsequent history of demonstrations and riots on campuses over the Viet Nam war, conflict over the issue of distributing leaflets and speaking out seems almost impossible to comprehend. This illustrates the pace of social change in the past decade.

REFERENCES

Anonymous. "Who Governs?" *Daily Californian* (Berkeley: University of California), 2 October 1974, p. 5.

Argyris, Chris. *Personality and Organization*. New York: Harper, 1957.

Arrow, Kenneth. *Social Choice and Individual Values*. New York: John Wiley, 1951.

Boulding, Kenneth, E. *The Organizational Revolution*. New York: Harper, 1953.

Calder, Bobby J.; Rowland, Kendrith M; and Leblebici, Huseyin. "The Use of Scaling and Cluster Techniques in Investigating the Social Structure of Organization." Faculty Working Paper #212. Urbana, Ill.: College of Commerce and Business Administration, University of Illinois, 1974.

Child, John. "Organization: A Choice for Man." In *Man and Organization*, edited by John Child, pp. 234-570. London: Halsted Press, 1973.

Crozier, Michel. *The Bureaucratic Phenomenon*. Chicago: University of Chicago Press, 1964.

Cyert, Richard M., and March, James G. *A Behavioral Theory of the Firm*. Englewood Cliffs, N.J.: Prentice-Hall, 1963.

Davis, Otto A.; Dempster, M.A.H.; and Wildavsky, Aaron. "A Theory of the Budgetary Process." *American Political Science Review 60* (1966): 529-47.

Dearborn, D. C., and Simon, H.A. "Selective Perception: A Note on the Departmental Identification of Executives." *Sociometry 21* (1958): 140-44.

Festinger, Leon. "A Theory of Social Comparison Processes." *Human Relations 7* (1954): 117-40.

Friedland, Edward I. *Introduction to the Concept of Rationality in Political Science*. Morristown, N.J.: General Learning Press, 1974.

Friedlander, F., and Pickle, H. "Components of Effectiveness in Small Organizations." *Administrative Science Quarterly 13* (1968): 289-304.

Galbraith, Jay. *Designing Complex Organizations*. Reading, Mass.: Addison-Wesley, 1973.

Gamson, William A. *Power and Discontent*. Homewood, Ill.: Dorsey Press, 1968.

Hickson, D. J.; Hinings, C. R.; Lee, C. A.; Schneck, R. E.; and Pennings, J. M. "A Strategic Contingencies Theory of Intraorganizational Power." *Administrative Science Quarterly 16* (1971): 216-29.

Homburger, Wolfgang S. "Case Study: San Francisco Bay Area Rapid Transit Planning and Development." In *Urban Mass Transit Planning*, edited by W. S. Homburger. Berkeley: Institute of Transportation and Traffic Engineering, University of California, 1967.

Kahn, Robert L.; Wolfe, Donald M.; Quinn, Robert P.; and Snoek, Diedrich J. *Organizational Stress: Studies in Role Conflict and Ambiguity*. New York: John Wiley, 1964.

Kelley, Harold H. *Attribution in Social Interaction*. Morristown, N.J.: General Learning Press, 1971.

Lasswell, Harold D. *Politics: Who Gets What, When, How*. New York: McGraw-Hill, 1936.

Mackenzie, Kenneth D. *Organizational Structures*. Arlington Heights, Ill.: AHM Publishing Corporation, 1978.

March, James G. "The Business Firm as a Political Coalition." *Journal of Politics* 24 (1962): 662-78.

Miles, Raymond E. *Theories of Management: Implications for Organizational Behavior and Development.* New York: McGraw-Hill, 1975.

Ouchi, William G., and Dowling, John B. "Defining the Span of Control." *Administrative Science Quarterly 19* (1974): 357-65.

Pettigrew, Andrew M. *The Politics of Organizational Decision-Making.* London: Tavistock, 1973.

Pfeffer, Jeffrey, and Leong, Anthony. "Resource Allocation in United Funds: Examination of Power and Dependence." *Social Forces 55* (1977): 775-790.

Pfeffer, Jeffrey, and Salancik, Gerald R. "Organizational Decision Making as a Political Process: The Case of a University Budget." *Administrative Science Quarterly 19* (1974): 135-51.

Salancik, Gerald R., and Pfeffer, Jeffrey. "The Bases and Use of Power in Organizational Decision Making: The Case of a University." *Administrative Science Quarterly 19* (1974): 453-73.

Schutz, A. *The Phenomenology of the Social World.* Evanston, Ill.: Northwestern University Press, 1967.

Scott, W. R.; Dornbusch, S. M.; Busching, B. C.; and Laing, J. D. "Organizational Evaluation and Authority." *Administrative Science Quarterly 12* (1967): 93-117.

Simmons, Richard E. *Managing Behavioral Processes: Applications of Theory and Research.* Arlington Heights, Ill.: AHM Publishing Corporation, 1978.

Smith, Peter B. *Groups Within Organizations.* London: Harper and Row, 1973.

Stagner, R. "Corporate Decision Making: An Empirical Study." *Journal of Applied Psychology 53* (1969): 1-13.

Thompson, James D. *Organizations in Action*. New York: McGraw-Hill, 1967.

Thompson, J. D., and Tuden, A. "Strategies, Structures, and Processes of Organizational Decision." In *Comparative Studies in Administration,* edited by J. D. Thompson, P. B. Hammond, R. W. Hawkes, B. H. Junker, and A. Tuden, pp. 195-216. Pittsburgh: University of Pittsburgh Press, 1959.

Tuggle, Francis D. *Organizational Processes*. Arlington Heights, Ill.: AHM Publishing Corporation, 1978.

Weber, M. *Theory of Social and Economic Organization*. New York: Oxford, 1947.

Weick, Karl E. *The Social Psychology of Organizing*. Reading, Mass.: Addison-Wesley, 1969.

Wolfe, Burton H. "Bart Probe." *The Bay Guardian*, June 18, August 30, November 1, and December 24, 1968.

Managing
Interdependence

Most considerations of organizational design ultimately derive from the interdependence that exists within organizations because of the division of labor that occurs among positions. One of the characteristics of modern organizations, large and small, is the division of labor into specialized roles—simply put, this means that different people do different things within an organization. Some people work on the production line, some handle finance, others are concerned with sales. Even within these broad areas there is division of labor until, on the assembly line, one person is responsible for only a few small parts of the total process of assembling a complex product such as an automobile or television. When the total task is broken up into smaller components, each of these smaller tasks must become interdependent with one another. Managing and coordinating this interdependence is achieved through the organization's structural arrangements. This is the central theme pursued by Thompson (1967, ch. 5) in his discussion of organizational structure. Thompson argued that structure developed to minimize coordination costs, which involved placing the most interdependent positions as close together as possible in the organization. Galbraith (1973), with his concern for information-processing considerations, also has emphasized the communication costs involved in coordinating interdependent activities.

One of the advantages of bureaucracy is the possibility of coordinating the effort of a large number of individuals, and thereby being able to accomplish things that are far beyond the capabilities of individuals or small, informal groups (Mackenzie, 1978, ch. 5). Bureaucracy represents the harnessing of a vast amount of human energy. Because any individual has limited information-processing capabilities and a limited set of skills, organizations use people to do only small parts of the total task. But differentiation of roles occurs even in small, informal groups. The emergence of task and socio-emotional leaders in experimental groups, and the differences in activities undertaken by participants in communication network experiments (e.g., Mackenzie, 1975), would seem to indicate that the division of labor is almost inevitable in social organizations. The division of labor makes specialization possible, and enables the total organization to overcome the bounded rationality that limits individual actors.

Differentiation occurs among organizations in the larger society, as well as within organizations. There are organizations concerned with education, others with health, and still others with the production of various goods and services. Organizations, like people, develop particular competencies, and the division of labor among organizations enables society as a whole to benefit from each organization's comparative advantage.

Specialization and the differentiation of roles within an organization present problems of coordinating the various activities and also raise difficulties for the control of behavior within the organization. In the simplest case, consider an organization of one person. In this instance, there are fewer coordination or control problems—one person does every task needed in the organization, there is no one to coordinate with, and further, the single-person organization can be sure the other organizational participants are committed to the same course of organizational action he is (of course, because there are not any other participants). As people are added to the organization, their activities must be coordinated. In addition, the issue of control appears—how can the person be sure that the new employees will act as he wants them to, will serve the organization's interests rather than their own (see Perrow, 1972, pp. 17-23), and will make decisions using organizationally relevant criteria.

To the extent that the people hired differ from each other in background, education, experience, and various social characteristics, the problems of coordination and control grow even more severe. Different education and experience implies different sets of socialization experiences, producing differences in terminology and perspective. We have already referred to the Dearborn and Simon (1958) study indicating the profound effect of location in the organization on problem definition. Similar effects exist for differences in terminology and criteria for decision-making, leading to greater coordination and control problems. Size and differentiation create control problems and at the same time provide advantages to the organization. The organizational design represents, at a given time, the resolution of these conflicting forces. In the rest of this chapter, we will examine some major dimensions of organizational design and examine how

they relate to the issue of organizational
control.

TASK AND ROLE SPECIALIZATION

From the time of the writings of Adam Smith
and his description of the manufacture of pins,
specialization has played an important part in
the design of work and tasks in organizations.
One premise has been that by giving someone a
relatively small part of the total task to do,
the person can become very skilled and profi-
cient at the one small set of activities,
thereby increasing his productivity. Specialization, in other words, presumably promotes
expertise. Specialization is now evident every-
where. The general practitioner in medicine is
becoming rare, and is actually now claiming
special status under the title of family medicine, as doctors specialize in ever more detailed and restricted areas of practice. A colleague of mine says that his family uses four
dentists: one for cleaning and filling, one for
extractions, one for root-canal work, and an
orthodontist to straighten his children's
teeth. Much of the process of education involves moving to successively greater depths of
knowledge in successively smaller areas of inquiry.

Specialization has recently come under attack
by the proponents of job enlargement or job
enrichment. These authors believe that the concern with task specialization has dealt only
with the cognitive and not the motivational aspects of work. Herzberg (1968), for example,
claimed that to motivate people one had to make
the work itself interesting and challenging.
The view was posed that specialization could
proceed too far, losing some benefits of expertise because of the lack of motivation
caused by the characteristics of the job. Re-
viewing the job enlargement literature is not
relevant here, and has been done by others in
any event (Hulin and Blood, 1968; Fein, 1974).

It is, however, important to note the possible consequences for motivation caused by job specialization.

From the point of view of analyzing power and control in organizations, specialization may have several effects. First, specialization can potentially make replacement easier, lessening the power of the position in the organization. Taking a large task and reducing it into smaller, relatively simple components should make it possible to hire persons more easily to do the small subtasks than to obtain persons to perform the entire job. Practically anyone can be trained to work at most stations on an automobile assembly line in a matter of hours, or days at the most. To find someone who could build an entire car would be substantially more difficult.

Specialization can lead to the decrease of power in a given position as specialization produces routinization in the task. The basic idea behind the concept of routinization is that elements are predictable and repeated— such as turning the bolts to put on a wheel, or soldering the same two wires together in the same place. Some tasks cannot be routinized—it is difficult to imagine routinizing the task of finding a cure for cancer, but even in this instance, some parts of the task can be routinized, such as cleaning up the laboratory or performing statistical analyses. It is generally the case that to routinize a task, one must divide it into its basic elements. This can be, then, the first step toward specialization, or the assigning of different people to do subparts of the total task. It is, however, also possible to have specialization without routinization. An artist may specialize in abstract art, landscapes, or portraits, but that does not mean that creating great art can be routinized.

Routinization of the task removes the uncertainty surrounding the performance of the task, and thereby reduces the power of those organizational members whose job involves performing

the task. This is because power derives from
the ability to cope with critical organizational uncertainties (Crozier, 1964; Hickson, et
al., 1971). Thus, specialization and routinization, when they threaten to alter the distribution of power in the organization, will be resisted by those who stand to lose control.
This general statement can provide partial explanation for the oft-documented resistance to
the implementation of management science or
operations research techniques and to the introduction of computers into organizations.

Specialization, by using different skills of
different people on different tasks, leads to
the increased likelihood of subgoal formation
in organizations, and also to increased coordination difficulties. March and Simon (1958) developed a model of how subgoal formation comes
about as a consequence of the division of labor
in organizations. Different subunits come to
pursue and value only their own activities,
fail to see their relationship with the entire
organization, and are therefore unable to make
decisions based on considerations relevant to
the total organization. This has been called
suboptimization. Similarly, the differentiation
of functions leads to the probability of more
conflict among the organizational members doing
different tasks and having different backgrounds and training. Dividing organizational
tasks into small components places a larger
burden of coordination on the management of the
organization.

The existing empirical literature on organizational structures indicates that the degree
of specialization and the degree of standardization or routinization of activities are
closely related (Pugh et al., 1968; Child,
1973a). Child (1972b) has called this the
bureaucratic strategy of organizational control, and has argued (Child, 1972b, 1973a,
1973b) that specialization, the standardization
and formalization of role activities, and the
centralization of decision-making are all related—the first two positively to each other

and both negatively to centralization. Further, the argument has been consistently and frequently made that size is one of the important factors causing the use of varying strategies of organizational control (Meyer, 1972; Child, 1973b). One aspect of this research that is troublesome is the implicit assumption that what is being varied is the mechanism for achieving organizational control, and not the total amount of control achieved. The authorities may be indifferent to the use of rules or anything else, as long as they can achieve control with the minimum expenditure of resources. Some of the research on structures neglects the differences in actual distributions of power and influence over organizational choices both across subunits and across hierarchical levels in different organizations.

We have discussed how specialization may lead to the routinization of tasks and thereby decrease the **power of a given** position, but this is not invariably the case. Specialization may also work to increase the power of a given position. One of the consequences of specialization is that there are fewer people in the organization who are familiar with a given role or set of activities. If everyone does the same thing, everyone is familiar with everyone else's job, and the switching of jobs is easy. If, however, tasks are specialized, there may be few organizational participants familiar with a particular task. If this task is also nonroutine, so it cannot be easily learned, the holder of the position responsible for the task comes to acquire additional control and influence because of the uniqueness of his skills within the organization. This suggests that the division of labor within an organization may either increase or decrease the influence of a given role, depending on whether the activities associated with that role can be analyzed and prescribed because of the routineness of the task.

Two examples serve to illustrate this point. The Zenith Radio Corporation manufactures

televisions in a plant in Chicago. Televisions
are complex electronic products: a given set
has a large number of circuits and components,
which must be precisely assembled. In this
case, the individual elements of the task can
be identified, and are repeated for every set.
Therefore, the company has organized the tasks
along an assembly line. At each position on
the line, a few simple operations take place,
such as the fastening together of a very few
wires or components. The tasks have been so
routinized that the company can introduce a
new model, requiring a completely different
assembly operation, in a matter of hours,
merely by reteaching the workers their simple
assembly tasks.

The consequences of this organization for
production is that any given worker has
little influence in the organization, and
even the workers as a group are relatively
powerless. Walk-ins off the street can
learn one of the tasks in a brief period
time, and consequently Zenith is not dependent on the workers to any large degree.

Contrast with this the organization of
medical practice. Here we find specialization, and indeed, increasing specialization
in treating specific illnesses or parts of
the body. But rather than decreasing the
specialist's influence, the greater division of labor has created a situation in
which persons doing very nonroutine and
complex tasks have relatively few competitors. In this instance, the division of
labor acts to increase the power and influence of the holders of the specialized
roles.

VERTICAL DIFFERENTIATION

In addition to horizontal specialization by
task, organizations also differ according to
the number of levels in the hierarchy. This
is occasionally referred to as the flatness or

tallness of the organizational structure. Organizational positions differ according to task, but they also differ according to the amount of authority and control possessed by the position's occupant. In an organization with two levels, there are two formally recognized distinctions in the amount of authority; in an organization with ten levels, ten different ranks, or amounts of control, are formally recognized. Even among peers, of course, differences in influence emerge (Blau, 1964), but the organizational hierarchy represents the formally constructed distinctions in authority and influence.

In addition to counting the number of levels on a formal organizational chart, the distribution of salary provides information about the amount of vertical differentiation in an organization (see, e.g., Whisler et al., 1967). In some organizations, automobile companies, for example, the highest paid member makes one hundred times what the lowest paid member makes. In other organizations, the difference between the highest and lowest paid member is on the order of nine or ten times. Whisler argued that the concentration of salary is a surrogate measure for the concentration of control. It is possible that persons having control will use it to extract relatively more resources from the organization, and the greater the difference in amount of power possessed, the greater the differences in salaries that will emerge. The use of control to ensure one's position in the contest for salary can be seen in many contexts. In Illinois, the pension system for state legislators is the only governmental pension system that is fully funded; in California, university administrators on occasion have given themselves nearly twice the raises provided to faculty members.

It is true that, controlling for the size of the organization and assuming a constant supervisorial span of control in the organization, there is a mathematical relationship between the number of hierarchical levels and the span

of control in the organization. The concept of
span of control refers to the number of persons supervised by any given supervisor (see
Mackenzie, 1978, ch. 4). The relationship between size, the number of levels, and the span
of control is:

$$X = \sqrt[n]{S}$$

where X is the span of control, n is the number
of levels in the hierarchy, and S is the number
of positions in the organization (see, e.g.,
Meyer, 1971).

Greater vertical differentiation, therefore,
may be associated with relatively smaller spans
of control, and also more supervision and closer
supervision over persons in the organization
(see Worthy, 1950; Mackenzie, 1978). Presumably,
with fewer people being supervised, and with
more levels of command in the structure, decisions are reviewed more, and there is greater
coordination and control of individual behavior
within the structure. As Mackenzie has noted,
the degree of hierarchy present in a structure
tends to be inversely related to the number of
untimely actions and redundant actions taken
(1978, ch. 1). Or, with greater hierarchical
control, there is more order and less wasted
activity in the organization's processes, provided that the task processes are efficient.

The idea that a narrow span of control is
required to control closely the behavior of organizational participants is not completely
correct. A narrow span of control is required
only when close control over personnel is desired *and* when this control must be interper-
sonally based. To the extent that behavior is
controlled by machines (Blau and Scott, 1962),
or by well-learned and easily monitored rules,
personal control is not necessary. As Mackenzie
has noted, the maximum possible span of control
is a function of factors including the routineness of the task being performed, and the time
required on the part of the supervisor to

monitor and coordinate the activities of the
people being supervised (1978, ch. 4). Thus,
the implicit assumption that a structure with
more levels, controlling for the total size
of the organization, means more control only
holds when we are comparing organizations with
similar tasks and similar degrees of interdependence among positions.

Indeed, increasing the number of levels in
the organization's hierarchy may even lead
to a decrease in control over behavior. This
is because information is often transmitted
following the formal structure. Most of us
have at one time or another played the game
where a message is whispered by one person to
the next, and then is passed around the room
by each person whispering the message to the
next until the end of the chain is reached.
We have all noticed how the message is distorted as it is passed, until what emerges at
the final position is frequently unrelated
to the original communication. Although organizations have the benefit of committing
the message to paper, it is nevertheless true
that as information flows through an organization, it is assimilated, summarized, filtered,
and distorted as it is communicated. Some of
this is unintentional, as perceptual biases
tend to make us hear what we expect and want
to hear. Some of the distortion is intentional,
as people attempt to manage information-flows
to place themselves in a favorable light. One
of the principal functions of staff groups of
high level executives is to find out what is
really going on. The filtering that took place
in the White House during the Nixon administration helped to make the Watergate break-in
and its coverup possible. While a narrow hierarchical structure provides more orderliness,
it also provides fewer alternative sources
of information, and the very control over the
organization that it provides may become
dysfunctional when change, adaptation, or
new information is required.

HORIZONTAL DIFFERENTIATION

Related to the concept of task specialization is horizontal differentiation. This concept has conventionally been measured by the number of departments (Meyer, 1972; Blau and Schoenherr, 1971), though Lawrence and Lorsch (1967) have emphasized that it is best measured by assessing the differences among departments in terms of structures, goal orientations, and time horizons. The effects of horizontal differentiation on control and influence are similar to the effects of task specialization. Indeed, one way of dividing the organization into departments is by task, so the greater the amount of specialization by task, the more departments there are likely to be.

Individuals are in organizational subunits. They come into contact with other workers primarily within their own unit, and are evaluated within that unit. Consequently, subunit identification is almost inevitable. Persons come to accept and identify with the subunit and its goals, and, over time, see other parts of their own organizations as adversaries in a contest for resources and control. Faculty members in a school of business identify with their subspeciality, be it finance or organizations, and within the university, identification with the department develops. Similarly, in business organizations, identification with the marketing department, finance department, or accounting department is likely to be observed if one talks to members of these departments. The greater the number of subunits, the greater the potential number of contestants for resources, and the greater the number of subgroups that can exist. As Lawrence and Lorsch suggested, horizontal differentiation imposes on the organization greater requirements for integrating the various units (1967). This integration task is more difficult the more subunits there are and the more different they are from each other.

Differentiation creates problems of control, as both Hall (1972) and Meyer (1972) have noted. However, the creation of parallel departments doing similar functions decreases the organization's dependence on any single unit, and therefore lessens the power of that subunit. Take the case of a conglomerate with 20 different lines of business, contrasted with another company which operates in only two markets, each with a different product. On the one hand, control problems will be more severe in the conglomerate, since there is great horizontal differentiation and a large number of very different departments to monitor. On the other hand, any given department is likely to be a small part of the organization's operation, and therefore will have relatively less influence. In the case of the two-department organization, although coordination is less of a problem and it is easier to monitor the subunits, it is also true that each subunit will have more influence within the organization. Thompson (1967) spoke to a related point when he wrote about the effects of decentralization. He noted that by creating more power positions the organization lessens its dependence on any one. Similarly, in the case of departments the creation of multiple departments increases the organization's problem of control, but the dependence on any single department is probably diminished. Of course, the amount of coordination required and the organization's dependence on a given subunit depend on the interdependence that exists within the organization.

The interdependence created by differentiation determines the relative power and influence distribution of subunits within the organization. In Hickson et al.'s (1971) model of subunit power, power is determined by: (a) the capability to cope with critical organizational contingencies, (b) the ability of other subunits to substitute for that coping capability, and (c) the pervasiveness or importance of the contingency for the organization. It should be obvious that the way the organization is subdivided allocates critical contingencies to various subunits, determines their interdependence with other subunits and with the organization's chance of task accomplishment, and we have just discussed how differentiation affects the issue of substitutability.

The relationship, then, between issues of organizational design and the control of organizational behavior should be increasingly clear. As discussed in the first chapter, design is involved in issues of the allocation of control in the organization. Although there are virtually no studies that have adopted this perspective in analyzing existing organizational structures, it does seem reasonable to presume that structural adjustments are undertaken with the knowledge of the implications for organizational influence and control. This position is certainly consistent with the argument of Child (1972a), who attributed the indeterminacy of much of the research investigating the relationships between organizational environments, technology, and structure to the neglect of the question of the power and strategy of the organizational managers.

We are left, then, with a similar conclusion for all dimensions of organizational differentiation—vertical and horizontal as well as task specialization: namely, that none is related in a simple fashion to the centralization or distribution of control or influence within the organization. Task specialization may increase the control of the authorities, if the tasks are routinized, or may increase the control of the task performer if the task is nonroutine and there are few others within the organization who can perform it. Vertical differentiation may provide increased orderliness and review of organizational processes, but by providing more levels between the top and bottom of the organization, it may cause so much distortion of information that control may

be lost rather than enhanced. And horizontal
differentiation, obtained through having a
large number of departments, may also lead to
different outcomes. On the one hand, greater
integration and control efforts may be required
as subunits develop subgoals and separate
identities. On the other hand, creation of
parallel units may lead to decreased reliance
on any single one, thereby lessening its influence within the organization.

It seems evident that these aspects of structure provide little unique information about
the influence and control of organizational actions. Further, these measures make a large
number of hidden assumptions about structures
(see Mackenzie, 1978). If control is a central
concern in organizational analysis, then the
utility of these aspects of structure for
understanding organizational action must be
questioned.

MANAGING INTERDEPENDENCE BY RULES

There are several alternative strategies for
coping with the interdependence created by the
division of labor within the organization, and
for maintaining control over the actions and
decisions made within the organization. Meyer
(1972), for instance, has distinguished between
control by personal supervision and control by
formal rules. In addition to these two strategies, there is also control by socialization
and control through admitting into the organization only those persons who can be relied on
to have decision premises similar to those of
the person seeking to attain or to maintain
control. We shall first consider interdependence management and control as accomplished
through the use of rules.

This aspect of organizational structure is
commonly referred to as the extent of formalization (Hall, 1972). It has typically been
measured by looking at whether or not there are

formal job descriptions (Hage and Aiken, 1969) or by the presence or absence of codified rules and procedures. Both March and Simon (1958) and Thompson (1967) recognized that rules could be used to coordinate behavior as long as the situation was stable. For example, consider the process of registration for classes at a university. The student goes to the department office, where a discrimination is made according to whether he is a graduate or undergraduate student. Then, a further discrimination may be made according to his field of specialization or major, and he is referred to the appropriate advisor or set of advisors. Each advisor is likely to have a catalogue or other document that specifies the required courses and admissible electives for a person pursuing such a degree or specialization, and also the student's own record. Courses in the area of study may require prerequisites, which are also specified. It is therefore possible for the advisor to help the student quickly develop a program of study for the coming academic period. Because of all the rules written down, no coordination was necessary with other instructors or persons in other areas of study. Prerequisites were specified, and the bulk of the student's required program was specified as well in advance. Although no individual differences or preferences are reflected in the rules, it is nevertheless true that it is easy to process a large number of such cases in a very short time without incurring costs of communication or coordination with anyone else.

But rules are more than ways of coordinating behavior without incurring repeated communication costs. Rules also tend to ensure that desired actions are taken. Persons do, of course, violate rules in their organizations, but, except in rare circumstances, such rule violation is likely to be exceptional rather than usual behavior. For most people most of the time, rules govern their actions and choices as the rules are relevant. Most students take a standard course of study, most employees follow

the requirements specified for their job, most
government employees follow the rules established for conducting their jobs, and so on.
When it is the end of the quarter, I give final
examinations and grades, regardless of how I
feel personally about either finals or grading.
We conform.

We conform because organizations have penalties for violating the rules, though the severity of the penalty varies with the importance
of the rule (possibly related to the amount of
loss of control), and the likelihood of its administration varies with the individual's personal power within the organization. Rule en-
forcement imposes a cost of surveillance. If I
have a rule that my employees must be at work
at 8:00, then to enforce that rule I must
establish time clocks or some other way of
monitoring the time at which people get to
work. If I have rules concerning eligibility
for food stamps, I must periodically audit the
decisions being made by the employees determining food stamp eligibility, to ensure that
they are acting within the rules and regulations. Since surveillance is costly, rule en-
forcement also has costs. However, since most
people most of the time obey the rules, formal
procedures still provide an easier way of dealing with interdependence than personal intervention in each case requiring a decision.

Formal procedures and rules are also useful
for avoiding conflict, because procedures develop as the outcome of past conflicts and experience, and serve as precedents to guide organizational behavior. Rules are standard operating procedures, and serve as the organization's memory (Cyert and March, 1963). When a
situation is confronted repeatedly, rules are
likely to emerge to deal with the situation.
For example, formal and elaborate procedures
for hiring are more likely to be found in an
organization where hiring decisions are frequently made. If the organization does little
hiring, either because it is small or because
turnover is very low, it is not likely to

develop procedures for coping with this infrequently encountered situation. Since most organizations encounter situations over time, it
is likely that rules and procedures will develop as the organization discovers what situations are either repeated frequently or are
particularly troublesome. The likelihood that
formalization increases over time because of
this effect provides an alternative hypothesis
to the finding that formalization is correlated
with organizational size (Meyer, 1972). Since
organizations grow over time also, the correla-
tion between formalization and time may be
partially spurious and a result of the relationship of both formalization and size to
time.

Since rules, once established, serve as precedents and guides to behavior, and are infrequently challenged, rules serve to handle situations in which conflict might otherwise arise.
For instance, consider the problem of allocating positions to departments in an organization. There is likely to be conflict over resources, and if this frequently requires a decision, such conflict is likely to recur frequently as well. In this instance, one frequently observed organizational response is to
develop a formal set of procedures for allocating positions. Once such rules and procedures
are accepted, future decisions can be made in
the context of the rules without engaging in as
much conflict and bargaining.

Rules, therefore, can be seen as analogous to
laws in the larger society. They form an organization's legal system, delimiting allowable
and nonallowable actions, and specifying the
criteria for making various organizational decisions. Rules confer legitimacy on actions
that might otherwise be questioned. In the case
of allocating positions, if there is a rule
that says there must be a certain ratio of
faculty to students, then the rule will govern
the decision situation. Only in exceptional
cases (as we will discuss in chapter 7) will
the rule itself be challenged. Most of the

time, the statement, "That's the rule in this
organization," is sufficient to carry the
argument.

Rules both limit behavior and provide freedom. Perrow (1972) is one of the few writers to
recognize this point. It is obvious how rules
limit freedom of action. What is not as ob-
bious is how rules provide freedom of action
to an organizational member. Rules provide
freedom because they limit the exercise of discretion by the authorities in organizations. If
there is a rule governing production quotas,
then as long as an employee meets the quota he
cannot be fired. In schools, there are rules
of academic eligibility. The rule that specifies a 1.75 grade-point average to graduate
means that a student must keep his average
above that level, but it also means that if a
student does maintain a sufficient average, he
cannot be denied the degree. Persons in organizations often seem to recognize implicitly this
function of formal rules, and frequently it is
the lower-level, less powerful participants who
seek rules and their protection. The asking of
what is required and how grades are computed on
the first day of class is one example of this
behavior.

Rules tend to homogenize members in an organization. Since all may be expected to conform to the same rules, differences in activities and in status may be somewhat reduced.
Rules, therefore, may reduce the special status
of expert members, and thereby reduce their
power. Excessive elaboration of rules can itself create confusion and uncertainty in the
organization. Such an outcome strengthens the
power of those thoroughly conversant with the
rules, the organizational quasilawyers.

Like laws, rules reflect the outcome of legislative battles in organizations. Rules reflect
the compromises made by organizational participants to resolve disagreements and disputes.
They serve as precedent as long as the power
structure that was in existence when they were
formed is stable, or as long as no group with

influence is so disadvantaged by their operation that it is worth reopening the dispute and
renegotiating the procedures and rules.

CENTRALIZATION

Rules provide protection for the less powerful organizational groups, and are a mechanism
of control that, in any event, is only suitable
when the situation is stable enough to make
rule-making a reasonable activity. When the
situation changes so frequently that rules are
always out of date, then rule-making is too
time-consuming to control behavior. Control administered through interpersonal mechanisms is
a substitute for rules that do not limit the
discretion of the authorities and can be altered as the situation changes. *Centralization*
has customarily referred to the extent to which
decision-making authority is concentrated in
the organization, where such concentration is
typically expected to occur at the higher organizational levels. *Centrality* (Mackenzie,
1978, ch. 6) has been defined in communication
networks in an analogous fashion--measuring the
extent to which a given position receives and
sends a greater than proportionally expected
number of messages. Mackenzie's research and
the research of the Aston group (Hinings et
al., 1974) both caution that centralization or
centrality measures may be different depending
on the decision issue or communication type we
are talking about. The concept is defined differently, however, by them. A given person may
be very central in communications about in-
formation-sharing, but occupy a much less central position when communications about formulation of solutions are considered. Similarly,
personnel decisions may be very decentralized
in organizations, while decisions governing the
allocation of resources may be highly centralized.

The levels in the organizational hierarchy
provide a mechanism for resolving conflicts and

achieving coordination (Thompson, 1967). When
there is disagreement among organizational
members at a given level, or when coordination
of activity on that level is required, one
solution is to establish a position having
authority over the others to make the final
decisions in case of disputes and to provide
for coordinated activity among them. Much as
in the case of rules, the possibility of ap-
pealing to a higher level in the organization
cools off the conflict among lower-level participants. In the case of rules, the rules have
legitimacy, and serve to enforce decisions that
are accepted. In the case of personal intervention, the organizational member in the
higher position has a certain degree of legitimacy because of his or her position, and can
arbitrate disputes and coordinate action among
subordinates because of this organizationally
derived authority. Centralization is a way of
resolving disputes and ensuring coordination.
Decisions and the responsibility of providing
direction are moved up in the organization.
Lower-level participants are told what to do,
and conflicts among them are decided by the
persons with more formal authority in the organization. Control is assured, since most decisions are being made only at the highest organizational levels. Mackenzie argued that
another job of those in the authority hierarchy
is to resolve issues when the authority is unclear (1978, ch. 2). This may be accomplished
by forming committees to ensure the requisite
authority.

While coordination and control by rules impose a cost of surveillance, coordination and
control accomplished through personal intervention impose costs of communication and decision-making time. Persons have limited information-processing capabilities. There are
only so many persons that can be coordinated,
and only so many decisions that can be made
before this capacity is exhausted. The possibility of information overload is real in centralized decision-making structures. In

Mackenzie's experiments using both complex "network decomposition" and a simple "minimum list of symbols" problems (1975; 1978, ch. 4), the person in the central role *and* the rest of the group were forced to move out of the centralized structure when the more complex task, with its greater problem-solving complexity and information-processing requirements, was encountered. Similarly, in formal structures there are limits to the extent decision-making and control can be centralized—limits determined by the nature of the task and the capabilities of the decision-maker.

One way of coping with the problem of overload is to decentralize those decisions and delegate those tasks that are less critical in maintaining control over the organization. Relatively unimportant decisions may be decentralized early, while control over critical issues such as the allocation of scarce and critical resources is maintained. In a university, for instance, even as such organizations have centralized, control over decisions such as the choice of textbooks, the staffing of courses, and the design of courses has remained with the departments. Control over the allocation of resources, such as positions and budget, however, has moved to higher levels in the hierarchy. When one cannot centralize everything, the most critical and important decisions are the focus of the centralization.

Centralization may lead to information overload and a slower response on the part of higher-level participants, but the most common response to external threat is centralization within the organization. Korten (1962) noted the tendency for nations faced with external threat to centralize, dispensing with many civil liberties and making decisions at the highest levels of government. Hamblin (1958), in an experimental study, found that leaders had more influence during crisis as opposed to noncrisis periods. Conceptualizing competition as a form of external threat, Pfeffer and Leblebici (1973) also found that the outcome

was an increased demand for organizational
control, leading to a more centralized decision-making structure. Because centralization ensures coordinated and controlled action,
taken consistent with the wishes of the authorities in the organization, centralization is
likely when a premium is placed on coordinated
behavior, when mistakes are very costly, and
when speed of response is important. Because
decisions are made in fewer positions in the
organization, a centralized decision-making
structure potentially can respond faster to external threats. Instead of having to consult
with the variety of persons responsible for
some part of an action, one person can quickly
make the decision and order it implemented if
the decision is centralized.

These results tend to indicate that decision-
making authority is delegated only to the extent required because of information-processing limitations or other constraints, and is
quickly recentralized under conditions of external threat or when the information-processing or other constraints can be overcome. One
constraint on centralization in addition to
information-processing limitations is the
legitimacy of the decision-making procedure.
Persons make contributions to organizations,
and expect to receive inducements at least
equal in value to the contributions made
(March and Simon, 1958, p. 84). Although some
inducements may be economic, persons are also
interested in organizational policies (Cyert
and March, 1963). Therefore, persons who contribute much to the organization are likely to
demand and expect more say in organizational
decisions. Such contributions may be in the
form of expertise or invested capital. The
outcome of this demand for more participation
in organizational decision-making may be a more
decentralized decision-making system.

If we consider only the case of invested
capital in business firms, the validity of the
argument seems apparent. We would expect more
centralized control, other things being equal,

in those firms in which ownership of stock is
more concentrated. Because of the concentration of investment in a few persons, there is
not the need or the pressure to share decision-
making authority as widely. A cursory consideration of American business firms supports
this argument. The proportion of outside directors is less, other things being equal, in
closely held firms. Moreover, the literature
on the history of various organizations also
supports the position that in firms with more
concentrated ownership, decision-making and
policy-setting have typically tended to be more
centralized in the hands of those having the
major ownership position (see Chandler, 1962).

The theme we will pursue throughout this book
emerges again in our discussion of centralization—namely, that the allocation of influence
in the organization is a political process
bound up with the process of control, and determined by the power various groups can bring
to bear to obtain greater control over the
organization. Concentration of power in the
hands of the authorities in a centralized organization is the natural state of affairs.
Decentralization must, therefore, result from
the loss of power by authorities—because they
need additional outside expertise, outside
financing, or some other resource that requires
an exchange with some other group. Centralization is a likely outcome of organizational
threats and crises, which provides a rationale
for legitimately reasserting claims to centralized control. If this is the case, then
crises are (occasionally) functional for organizational leaders in the same way that they
are functional for national political leaders—
the crisis provides a setting in which it is
easier to obtain centralized control over the
organization or nation. Just as national leaders have, then, occasionally been accused of
either manufacturing external crises or else
interpreting events as a crisis, so we would
expect the dominant coalition in an organization to use external threat or the

interpretation of external events to buttress
its claim to centralized control and authority.
This point is important and should be kept in
mind when we discuss the organization of a
university in chapter 8.

THE PARADOX OF DECENTRALIZED CENTRALIZATION

Centralization, the personal control of organizational decisions, involves the obtrusive
use of organizational power. The abrogation of
decision-making authority, particularly in an
organization populated with professionals or
highly skilled personnel, is likely to be re-
sented, and cause opposition to the form and
method by which decisions are made. Indeed,
the visibility of power and control that ac-
companies centralized decision-making may be
as powerful an argument against it as the problem of information and decision overload.

Fortunately, however, the institution of full
and complete participation in organizational
decision-making can, under certain circumstances, lead to a situation of as much centralized control without the appearance of
centralization. Consider a subunit (or an organization) with 50 or so members, of more or
less equal rank and skills. A university department, a research and development laboratory, a large operations-research group, a law
or accounting firm, a large marketing research
or planning department—any of these fits this
description. Further, consider a decision which
is frequently made, such as the allocation of
budget, the hiring of new members, or the
evaluation of present personnel. Under a centralized decision-making system, there might
be one person, the department head, who makes
these decisions, or at most a small group of
advisors. This situation may lead to demands
for greater participation. If the organization
goes to a system of full and complete participation, with each person's opinion equally
weighted, it is reasonable to predict, following Michel's Iron Law of Oligarchy, that

again a centralized decision-making system will develop. Since it will be centralized under the guise of decentralization, the decision-making will be, in fact, even more centralized than before, because it will be difficult to fix accountability and opposition for decisions on any person.

Centralized decision-making will recur because first, the organizational participants are likely to be too busy with their own tasks to involve themselves extensively in these administrative functions. Second, while participation in decision-making can be widely dispersed, it is difficult to conceive of a situation where information-gathering and contacts with other subunits and the environments are also tasks that are widely shared. Thus, participants will be reacting to options that have been prepared by some person or small subgroup. One cannot develop proposals in a large committee, as recent legislative experience in Congress has demonstrated. Thus, in operation, there will still be a filtering of input to the decentralized decision-making structure, and within that structure, there will probably be some reluctance to participate fully in various decisions because of the time involved. As a consequence, responsibility for recruiting candidates, or allocating budget, or evaluation, or whatever will be explicitly or implicitly delegated to a much smaller group. Particularly in the case of implicit delegation, the principle becomes "who is willing to take on this task?" The consequence for decision-making outcomes is clear. The person or persons having done the task will have some claim to the legitimacy of their decision, since they will argue that the other participants shirked their responsibility. Further, since the larger group will still be reacting to proposals and dealing with information developed in a centralized structure, much of the variance in possible outcomes will have already been eliminated.

What this suggests is that the opposite of centralization is not complete participation by all organizational members, which is likely to result in a decision system that operates in a centralized fashion even though it is called something else. Instead, as a coalition model of organizations would suggest, the opposite of centralization is participation in the decision-making and alternative-formulating and information-gathering activities by persons representing the various interests within the social group. Representation of the various interests and points of view seems to be what is sought, but the consequence of a system presuming full participation by a large number is more likely to result in a system concentrated in a very few hands.

Although we have named this section after the paradox of decentralized centralization, there is really no paradox if you think of the organization as having a number of structures. The centrality of the sum of these structures is always less than or equal to the centrality of the parts. Thus, we can think of a simple case in which there is a completely centralized decision-making structure, and a completely decentralized, all-channel ratification or discussion structure. While the combined structure may appear to be decentralized, the decision-making structure is actually quite centralized.

RECRUITMENT AND SOCIALIZATION

In addition to the use of rules and personal intervention, control and coordination can be achieved through the organizational processes of recruitment and socialization. In these latter processes, organizational control is maintained not by surveillance or personal action, but by ensuring that organizational participants will act in the way desired by the authorities, either because they have been selected for their willingness and ability to do so, or because they have been trained to act in conformity with the authorities' preferences.

Organizational members may be selected by many criteria. Typically, our society values use of criteria related to individual merit, and favors the use of objective standards of assessment uniformly applied. However, much of the recruitment and hiring that takes place tends to differentially favor persons at different points in a social network, and often rewards loyalty and conformity above performance or other such standards. The operation of "old boy" networks of hiring exist in industry and government, as well as in academe, where they are endemic (Caplow and McGee, 1958). This system of hiring uses social contacts both to find candidates and to evaluate them for hiring. Obviously, one's likelihood of getting hired depends on one's position in the social network, or the relationships with the persons doing the hiring or the referring. These particularistic hiring and recruitment systems are presumably incompatible with the bureaucratic standards of evaluation based on merit and decision-making in agreement with total organizational objectives. Yet, such idiosyncratic behavior persists.

If we consider the objective of the authorities as control rather than some vaguely defined notion of organizational effectiveness or performance, the general basis for the observed hiring and recruitment patterns makes much more sense, and we can even derive some hypotheses concerning their use. If my objective is control of the organization, then ability and merit are certainly useful qualities to seek, but are luxuries easily dispensed with because: (a) they are qualities which are frequently very difficult to measure, and (b) they may not do as much for my acquisition of power and influence as qualities such as loyalty and trustworthiness. Indeed, subordinates with too much merit may actually pose a threat to my position of control and authority. On the other

hand, recruiting persons similar to me in
background probably assures my obtaining someone with similar viewpoints and objectives, as
well as ensuring at least some minimal social
connections. Since attraction is related to
social similarity (Berscheid and Walster, 1969),
I can be fairly certain that I will possess
some degree of referent power (French and
Raven, 1968). Hiring through the social network minimizes the risk of obtaining a deviant,
and is consistent with the desire to enhance
control in the organization. If necessary,
loyalty and willingness to follow directions
can be further imposed as criteria for the
hiring process.

The process we have described is somewhat
confounded by the fact that since we tend to
think most highly of people who are similar to
us, the person, confronted with his behavior,
may maintain sincerely that he has attempted to
hire the "best" people, but it happens that
the "best" people all are like him (the possibility of ego enhancement in this process is
obvious). Yet there are clear cases when the
recruitment process is based on criteria more
directly related to the maintenance of control
than to performance. Loyalty, possession of
similar values and criteria, and social similarity should be more important criteria in
recruiting when the contest for control is
more problematic, when objective standards of
evaluation are unavailable, and when the outcomes of the contest for control are scarce and
critical to those contesting for the control.
Thus, for example, loyalty to those in authority should be used more in recruitment when the
organization anticipates a proxy fight or some
other form of contest for control. Similarly,
loyalty and social similarity may be more important when the contest for control has as its
outcome the control over resources such as
positions or funds that are quite scarce and
critical.

As a substitute for recruitment, socialization may be employed to mold the values and

preferences of organizational participants
brought into the organization. Instead of
screening for loyalty, social similarity, or
similarity in values, these may be inculcated
once the employee is in the organization. One
of the more effective ways of ensuring a conformity of interests is by giving the employee
or participant some stake in the control process and its outcomes. In organizations, this
is done through patronage, which, believe it
or not, exists in business firms as well as in
the city of Chicago. By bargaining future rewards for present alliances, the authorities
use the promise of future benefits to ensure
their position in the present. Patronage, of
course, has costs (Wilson, 1961), the most
evident one being the use of resources or rewards. Further, the process involves bargaining
away future flexibility for present commitments. Nevertheless, as the experience in government indicates, patronage can produce a system that is stable and enduring.

Socialization is accomplished through personal contact, by telling the employee what is
expected, and by providing incentives for him
to behave in conformity with these expectations. Once behavior has been exhibited, attitudes and values are likely to follow. There
is a process of inculturation that goes on in
all groups and organizations (see, e.g., Jacobs
and Campbell, 1961), as new participants are
trained in the ways and attitudes of the existing culture. Organizational training programs provide socialization as well as other
forms of training, and things such as uniforms,
stock ownership, organizational newspapers,
company social events, and attempts to communi-
cate the prestige of the organization, all
serve to bind the employee more closely to the
organization.

Much as in the case of recruitment, we might
expect that attempts to socialize persons to
ensure loyalty to subgroups or persons within
the organization would be greater when there
was more active struggling for control, and

when the consequences of the struggle were
more important. Socialization or recruitment
to produce loyalty is less necessary when there
is less of a threat to the position of the
authorities.

LEADERSHIP AS INTERDEPENDENCE MANAGEMENT

Throughout this chapter we have emphasized
the importance of the interdependence that
exists between tasks and positions within the
organization. The division of labor and resulting interdependence creates problems of
control and coordination that must be solved
by those in the dominant coalition in a bureaucracy in order to assure that the organization
will operate effectively seeking the goals of
this group. We have noted that this coordination and control may be provided through the
use of formal rules and procedures, through
personal intervention in decision-making, or
through the use of recruitment and socialization processes. We conclude this chapter by ex-
tending our discussion to the role of the leader or supervisor (see Simmons, 1978).
    If the organization is thought of as a coali-
tion of interests and subunits, then one important function for the leader of a given group
or subunit is to manage its relationships with
the rest of the organization. Since the subunit
is interdependent with others in the organization, the role of the leader becomes managing
this interdependence so as to enhance the
group's or subunit's position vis à vis others
in the organization. This view of leadership is
not very different from some earlier approaches. Bavelas (1960) defined leadership in
terms of the functions the leader was expected
to perform. He noted that these functions were
dispersed throughout the group, and therefore
it made more sense to ask about the allocation
of functions over group members than to ask who
is the leader. Mackenzie's (1978) research on
group structures also emphasizes the

distribution of functions over group members.
Hollander and Julian (1969) summarized much of
the leadership literature by noting the similarity to the concepts of power and influence.
Clearly, the functions performed by group members are not equally critical or important.
Those doing the more important functions, or
coping with the more critical contingencies,
come to have more influence, and come to be
identified as the leaders. It is our position
that one of the most critical problems confronting the group is negotiating its relationships with other subunits within the organization. Thus the role of leadership is identified
with the task of interdependence management.

   There are several strategies that leaders
pursue both to ensure their position within
their own subunit and to enhance their subunit's position in the total organization. One
such strategy uses the formal rules and procedures of the organization. It is usually the
case that over time a variety of rules are developed in formal organizations. It is also the
case that few organizational members have either the interest or the time to familiarize
themselves thoroughly with these various procedures. Thus, one model of subunit enhancement
involves the leader's learning and using the
formal rules. We might call this strategy that
of the organizational lawyer. Because of the
legitimacy and general acceptance of rules,
the strategy can be quite effective. Further,
since few systems of law or rules are developed
that do not contain some ambiguities and internal contradictions, there is the opportunity
for successful advocacy of almost any position.
The organizational lawyer, in his use of the
rules selectively to favor his position, is
likely to evoke counterattacks with similar
strategies by the leaders of other subunits.
However, unlike the formal legal system, internal organization rules seldom specify the
conditions of their use in an adversary proceeding. If time for making the decision is
short, the well-prepared organizational lawyer

may carry the day simply because his opponents do not have the time to muster a successful defense using the formal organizational rules.

Knowing organizational procedures is obviously a source of power. It may account for the prominence of lawyers in many management positions in organizations, and almost certainly accounts for the influence of the administrative assistants, those relatively low-level employees who have been in the organization for years and know every nuance and subtlety concerning the operation of the formal bureaucracy. The importance of knowing parliamentary rules for winning Congressional battles is also well known. The procedures, once established, act much as the law in a society, capable of being used by those skillful and clever enough to advance their interests and the interests of their subunit.

A more straightforward method of enhancing the subunit's position derives from the fact that power is a function of the relative dependence between the subunit and the rest of the organization (see Emerson, 1962). If the subunit can increase the organization's dependence on it or increase its critical position for the organization, it will be able to have more influence in organizational operations. At the same time, if the subunit can reduce its dependence on other subunits within the organization, it can further enhance its power.

A subunit may increase its independence of other subunits within the organization by obtaining independent access to resources. For instance, in a university, outside grants and contracts provide departments and other research units with access to resources that are not contingent on the actions of other subunits or the administration. Operations research or other management consulting services within a firm may develop clients outside of the host organization, similarly obtaining resources outside of the parent organization. Subunits may develop independent recruiting and

training programs, ensuring access to personnel
resources without having to depend on other
departments within the organization, and similarly, other localized boundary-spanning functions such as marketing or public relations may
be developed. One resource of importance is
information, as we will discuss in more detail
in the next chapter. The issue of whether the
subunit has or does not have its own computer
and information system also becomes critical
for its power in the organization.

A subunit may increase the dependence of
other subunits on itself by: (a) either making
its present activities and resources appear
more critical to the rest of the organization,
or (b) undertaking activities or obtaining resources important to other subunits within the
organization. To the extent that the subunit
can define the organization's critical problems
as falling within its area of competence, its
influence in the organization will be enhanced.
Similarly, organizational subunits may, on occasion, actually create contingencies for the
organization that it can then resolve. The industrial relations department needs a certain
amount of labor unrest in order to maintain
a position of influence, and similarly, if production problems do not occur occasionally, the
importance of that department may be taken for
granted. Subunits and their leaders strategically use crises to enhance their own interests
within the organization. Once again, as in the
case of the organization lawyer, there will be
countervailing opposition. Successful leadership, however, involves acquiring important
functions and defining ambiguous situations
in ways that favor the importance, and therefore the power, of the subunit.

The division of labor, the interdependence
it creates, and the formal procedures designed
to coordinate the interdependence, provide subunit leaders with the opportunity to enhance
the position of their group within the total
organization. If one of the key elements in
organizations is the contest for control, then

leadership itself must be related to this process, and related to the use of rules, procedures, strategic resources, and crises in obtaining increased power and influence.

REFERENCES

Bavelas, Alex. "Leadership: Man and Function." *Administrative Science Quarterly 4* (1960): 491-98.

Berscheid, Ellen, and Walster, Elaine. *Interpersonal Attraction*. Reading, Mass.: Addison-Wesley, 1969.

Blau, Peter M. *Exchange and Power in Social Life*. New York: John Wiley, 1964.

Blau, Peter M., and Schoenherr, Richard A. *The Structure of Organizations*. New York: Basic Books, 1971.

Blau, Peter M., and Scott, W. Richard. *Formal Organizations*. San Francisco: Chandler, 1962.

Caplow, Theodore, and McGee, Reece. *The Academic Marketplace*. New York: Basic Books, 1958.

Chandler, Alfred D., Jr. *Strategy and Structure*. Boston: MIT Press, 1962.

Child, John. "Organizational Structure, Environment and Performance: The Role of Strategic Choice." *Sociology 6* (1972a): 2-22.

_____. "Organization Structure and Strategies of Control: A Replication of the Aston Study." *Administrative Quarterly 17* (1972b): 163-77.

_____. "Strategies of Control and Organizational Behavior." *Administrative Science Quarterly 18* (1973a): 1-17.

_____. "Predicting and Understanding Organization Structure." *Administrative Science Quarterly 18* (1973b): 168-85.

Crozier, Michel. *The Bureaucratic Phenomenon*. Chicago: University of Chicago Press, 1964.

Cyert, Richard M., and March, James G. *A Behavioral Theory of the Firm*. Englewood Cliffs, N.J.: Prentice-Hall, 1963.

Dearborn, D. C., and Simon, H. A. "Selective Perception:

A Note on the Departmental Identification of Executives." *Sociometry 21* (1958): 140–44.

Emerson, Richard M. "Power–Dependence Relations." *American Sociological Review 27* (1962): 31–41.

Fein, M. "Job Enrichment: A Reevaluation." *Sloan Management Review 15* (1974): 69–88.

French, John R. P., Jr., and Raven, Bertram. "The Bases of Social Power." In *Group Dynamics*, edited by Dorwin Cartwright and Alvin Zander, pp. 259–69. New York: Harper and Row, 1968.

Galbraith, Jay. *Designing Complex Organizations*. Reading, Mass.: Addison–Wesley, 1973.

Hage, Jerald, and Aiken, Michael. "Routine Technology, Social Structure and Organizational Goals." *Administrative Science Quarterly 14* (1969): 366–77.

Hall, Richard H. *Organizations: Structure and Process*. Englewood Cliffs, N.J.: Prentice–Hall, 1972.

Hamblin, R. L. "Leadership and Crises." *Sociometry 21* (1958): 322–35.

Herzberg, Frederick. "One More Time, How Do You Motivate Workers?" *Harvard Business Review 46* (1968): 53–62.

Hickson, D. J.; Hinings, C. A.; Lee, C. A.; Schneck, R. E., and Pennings, J. M. "A Strategic Contingencies' Theory of Intraorganizational Power." *Administrative Science Quarterly 16* (1971): 216–29.

Hinings, C. R.: Hickson, D. J.; Pennings, J. M.; and Schneck, R. E. "Structural Conditions of Intraorganizational Power." *Administrative Science Quarterly 19* (1974): 22–44.

Hollander, Edwin P., and Julian, James W. "Contemporary Trends in the Analysis of Leadership Processes." *Psychological Bulletin 71* (1969): 387–97.

Hulin, Charles L., and Blood, Milton R. "Job Enlargement, Individual Differences and Worker Responses." *Psychological Bulletin 69* (1968): 41–55.

Jacobs, Robert C., and Campbell, Donald T. "The Per-
petuation of an Arbitrary Tradition through Successive
Generations of a Laboratory Microculture." *Journal of
Applied Social Psychology 62* (1961): 649–58.

Korten, David C. "Situational Determinants of Leadership Structure." *Journal of Conflict Resolution 6*
(1962): 222–35.

Lawrence, Paul, and Lorsch, Jay. *Organization and Environment*. Boston: Division of Research, Harvard
Business School, 1967.

Mackenzie, Kenneth D. *A Theory of Group Structures*.
London: Gordon and Breach, 1975.

———. *Organizational Structures*. Arlington Heights,
Ill.: AHM Publishing Corporation, 1978.

March, James G., and Simon, Herbert A. *Organizations*.
New York: John Wiley, 1958.

Meyer, Marshall W. "Some Constraints in Analyzing Data
on Organizational Structures." *American Sociological
Review 36* (1971): 294–97.

———. *Bureaucratic Structure and Authority*. New York:
Harper and Row, 1972.

Perrow, Charles. *Complex Organizations: A Critical Essay*. Glenview, Ill.: Scott, Foresman, 1972.

Pfeffer, Jeffrey, and Leblebici, Huseyin. "The Effect
of Competition on Some Dimensions of Organizational
Structure. *Social Forces 52* (1973): 268–79.

Pugh, D. S.; Hickson, D. J.; Hinings, C. R.; and Turner,
C. "Dimensions of Organization Structure." *Administrative Science Quarterly 13* (1968): 65–105.

Simmons, Richard E. *Managing Behavioral Processes:
Applications of Theory and Research.* Arlington Heights,
Ill.: AHM Publishing Corporation, 1978.

Thompson, James D. *Organizations in Action*. New York:
McGraw-Hill, 1967.

Whisler, T. L.; Meyer, H.; Baum, B. H.; and Sorensen,
P. F., Jr. "Centralization of Organizational Control:

An Empirical Study of Its Meaning and Measurement."
Journal of Business 40 (1967): 10-26.

Wilson, James Q. "The Economy of Patronage." *Journal of
Political Economy 69* (1961): 369-80.

Worthy, James C. "Factors Influencing Employee Morale."
Harvard Business Review 28 (1950): 61-73.

Information Systems

We have argued that organizational structures are, in part, outcomes of a contest for influence and control that occurs in organizations. Three sets of variables affect the relationship between control and possible organizational structures: (1) information technology and the information system of the organization, (2) the organization's technology, and (3) the environment in which the organization operates. Each of these affects the distribution of influence within the organization, as well as the technology and possibility for maintaining control over members' behavior. We will consider each factor in turn, beginning with an examination of the role of information systems and information technology.

Organizational information systems and information technology are important adjuncts to the process of organizational control and governance. Indeed, one way of measuring structure is through mapping the communication flows in organizations, an extension of the literature on small group networks (Bavelas, 1950; Leavitt, 1951; and Mackenzie, 1975). Information is required to control behavior, and the possession of information can provide influence to persons in the organization. Information is necessary to engage in organizational actions, and the control of information in organizations is one important but unexplored method of maintaining and enhancing influence in a social structure. Information technology, particularly computer technology, enhances the information-processing capability of persons, leading to possible alterations in the systems of control and governance.

INFORMATION TECHNOLOGY AND CENTRALIZATION

No topic has sparked more debate, with perhaps less enlightenment, than the possible effect of computers on centralization, or the vertical distribution of control in organizations. The 1950s saw a number of articles attempt to forecast the effects of computers on management, with one common focus the impact of computers on the distribution of control (e.g., Leavitt and Whisler, 1958; Simon, 1960; Hoos, 1960).

The basic argument was that decentralization came about because of the information-processing constraints of decision-makers. Much as a division of labor resulted from the inability of a single person to be competent at all organizational tasks, so decentralization, it was thought, came about because of the information-processing limitations of managers. A given person could make only so many decisions and process so much information. When the capacity of the manager was exceeded, in order to maintain organizational functioning, some of the decisions would have to be given to others in the organization—frequently, delegated down to subordinate positions. Following this line of argument, it was thought that information technology would enhance the capabilities of managers, permitting a recentralization of control and a general moving of decisions to higher levels in the organizational hierarchy. The most common forecast was for computerization to lead to more centralized organizational structures.

However, a counter argument could also be made. Burlingame (1961), and subsequently, Pfeffer and Leblebici (1977), maintained that advanced information technology could facilitate the decentralization of organizational structures. These authors noted that with computers, feedback on performance and organizational processes could be more complete, more accurate, and more rapid. Whereas one might have been unwilling to delegate decision-making before, now with an information system that collected large amounts of data on performance, delegation might be possible. If the decisions being made were not to the manager's liking, he could find out accurately and rapidly the consequences of the decisions, and then take corrective action. This part of the argument, then, held that people were more likely to permit subordinates to make decisions when feedback concerning those decisions could more rapidly be provided.

Furthermore, it was argued that information technology might facilitate the evaluation of outcomes rather than processes. As will be discussed in more detail later in this chapter, the control process can proceed either by assessing the behavior, activities, or way the job is done, or by examining the results or outcomes, or some combination of the two. In the absence of outcome information, it is probably necessary to monitor the way in which the job is done. In this instance, it is probably almost as easy to do the job oneself, particularly when the task is decision-making. When, however, outcome data become available rapidly and accurately through more developed computer systems, process evaluation can give

way to outcome evaluation, and subordinates
may be permitted to make decisions, since the
consequences of such decisions can now be more
adequately assessed.

The empirical evidence of the effect of information technology on centralization is
mixed. Whisler (1970), in a study of insurance
companies, reported that information technology
led to increased centralization. But Whisler
also reported that the introduction of information technology led to a decrease in employment
in the organizations. Since large size is
negatively correlated with centralization (see
Child, 1973), the relationship between information technology and centralization Whisler
found could be a consequence of decreasing
size. In an analysis of 37 small manufacturing
companies, Pfeffer and Leblebici (1977)
found that, with size statistically controlled,
there was a negative relationship between information technology and centralization, or the
greater the use of information technology, the
more decentralized organizations were. Unfortunately, the two studies are not comparable
either in terms of the measures of centralization or, more importantly, in terms of the type
of organizations examined.

Even more troublesome is the following conceptual issue. When discretion is apparently
delegated in an organization, because outcomes
and organizational activities can be rapidly
and accurately assessed, does this constitute
real decentralization? Decentralization, as
assessed, for example, by Whisler et al.,(1967)
has come to refer to the distribution of control in organizations throughout the organizational hierarchy. If persons are allowed discretion, but are permitted the opportunity to
make decisions because their performance can
be rapidly and accurately assessed, it seems
that there has been no real sharing of control,
influence, or power in the organization. It is
conceivable, then, that the introduction of information technology can make possible the appearance of decentralization while maintaining

effective centralized control over organizational operations. This is accomplished through
the apparent delegation of decision-making authority, but at the same time implementing information systems that provide organizational
authorities with comprehensive information
on performance. Since participation and decentralization have generally been thought to be
motivators, at least for many employees, the
organization is in the position of attaining
the motivational benefits of decentralization
while still maintaining actual control over
organizational activities.

Effective control can be maintained with information technology even though more apparent
discretion is allowed organizational members.
Depending on the measure employed, the introduction of computers may lead to greater centralization or decentralization. But in terms
of effective organizational control, or in
terms of the distribution of influence within
the organization, the most likely outcome is an
increased concentration of power.

INFORMATION TECHNOLOGY AND DIFFERENTIATION

Hall (1972) has summarized the argument
that increased differentiation, either more
subunits or more levels in the organizational
hierarchy, tends to lead to more problems of
organizational control and coordination.
Lawrence and Lorsch (1967) have argued that increased differentiation, measured by differences in goals, structures, and time orientations among subunits, leads to greater need
for integration and coordination. More hierarchical levels can lead to more distortion in
information as it moves through the organization. Both problems, of coordination and information, can be lessened with information
technology. By enhancing the information-han-
dling capacity of managers, more subunits can be
effectively coordinated per manager, *ceteris
paribus*. By providing for the rapid and accurate

collection and transmission of information, information technology can overcome some of the distortions that tend to occur when information is passed from participant to participant. Other things being equal, then, information technology should permit the development of more elaborate and complex organizational structures.

In the study mentioned earlier, Pfeffer and Leblebici observed a positive relationship between information technology and both the number of departments and the number of organizational levels, when size was controlled. These findings again are different from those reported by Whisler in his study of insurance companies. However, as in the case of centralization, both the number of departments and the number of levels are related to organizational size (Meyer, 1972). Because Whisler did not control for the effect of size in his analysis, it is not possible to assess whether his results are different from those in the study of the small manufacturing organizations.

Although it seems clear that information technology permits the use of more complex and differentiated structures, information technology itself is not likely to cause such structures. Environmental heterogeneity and change (Lawrence and Lorsch, 1967), which have been hypothesized to be related to organizational differentiation, are more likely to lead to such differentiation when the organization has information systems that enable the resulting complex structures to be managed.

Information technology makes the management of complex structures more feasible, but it also makes differentiation less necessary. Recall that one of the reasons for the division of labor in organizations was limitations in cognitive capacity (see, e.g., Thompson, 1967, p. 54). With computer technology, such information-processing constraints are reduced, potentially permitting less division of labor among managers and other organizational personnel. Consider, for example, the tasks of

production-scheduling and inventory control in
a manufacturing plant producing several products. Without computer assistance, separate
persons may have to perform the production-
scheduling and monitoring of the inventory for
each of the products. Information technology
may permit the combination of these tasks into
fewer positions, using computer programs to
monitor inventory and schedule production for
the entire range of products.

Thus, the implementation of information
technology in an organization may have several
effects, some of which offset each other. On
the one hand, by enhancing the information-
processing capacities of managerial personnel,
more complex and differentiated structures can
be successfully coordinated and controlled.
This effect was observed by Pfeffer and
Leblebici (1977). On the other hand, by
generally increasing the information-processing capacity of positions in the organization,
the implementation of information technology
may make less division of labor and task specialization necessary in the organization.

EVALUATIONS AND REWARDS

Organizational evaluations, and the administration of rewards or punishments based upon
these evaluations, are important components of
the organization's authority system (Scott et
al., 1967), and affect the distribution of influence within the organization. Scott and his
colleagues have noted that positions in the organization may be authorized to undertake any
or all of the four steps in the evaluation process with respect to some other position: assigning of tasks, establishing criteria, sam-
pling performance, and assessing the sampled
performance by the criteria. The concept of
authorization means that it is generally accepted in the organization that such authority
rights are possessed by the position in question. If organizational rewards are important

to the participants, and if rewards are based,
at least partly, on the evaluations of performance, then the right to evaluate provides
power to the person possessing that right.

Evaluations may be based on an assessment of
the process or activities by which the job is
done, or by an assessment of the outcome of
the process. Salespeople are most frequently
evaluated by the amount of merchandise sold,
an outcome measure, not by the quality of the
sales presentation or their level of effort.
It is likely that outcome measures are pre-
ferred in evaluation but cannot always be
used. Occasionally, outcomes are interdependent on the performance of a large number of
persons, and rewarding a single person for the
total outcome may not accurately reflect his
level of performance. Also, occasionally outcome measures are difficult to specify, or
else very difficult to measure. In the class-
room, for instance, the desired outcome is
learning the course material. Theoretically,
this could best be assessed by measuring the
students' knowledge of the material before and
after taking the course. In the absence of
standardized tests or well-defined knowledge
objectives, process measures tend to be employed in evaluating teaching effectiveness.
Typical course evaluation questions on surveys
deal with the availability of the instructor
outside of class, the extent to which the instructor is prepared and gives organized lec-
tures, and other questions which assess the
process, but not the outcome, of the instructional process.

Process evaluation is typically interpersonal
in nature. It is difficult to develop forms
or computer systems that assess the process
by which a job is done. Conversely, outcome
measures can be implemented using information
technology, and indeed, information technology
facilitates the collection of a multitude of
outcome measures, and their comparison and
summarization. Consequently, information technology, we can argue, facilitates the use of

outcome-oriented evaluations, which is typically a less personal means of control. Outcome
measures appear objective, require less direct
supervision, and decrease the visibility of
power and authority in the organization. This
is beneficial since persons typically prefer
not to feel directly controlled and supervised.
Although information technology is helpful in
implementing outcome evaluations, such measures
are more difficult to employ when there is
great interdependence among many positions involved in determining some result, or when the
connections between actions and outcomes are
uncertain.

Information technology also permits the en-
forcement of rules and the monitoring of behavior to ensure that suboptimization, or attention to subgoals of organizational subunits,
will not occur. Rules and procedures must be
enforceable in order to have any effect on behavior in the organization, unless they also
serve to reduce the uncertainty of the persons
doing the tasks. Information technology enhances the possibility of monitoring compliance
with procedures and rules, and therefore can
make the implementation of formalized procedures more possible. At the same time, however,
because of the ability to obtain accurate and
rapid feedback on organizational performance,
the implementation of rules and procedures is
less necessary, since behavior need not be as
directly and immediately controlled to ensure
the same level of total organizational control.
In the study of the small manufacturing organizations, Pfeffer and Leblebici found a negative
relationship between information technology and
formalization. This result would indicate that
information technology, by providing the capability for processing more information on organizational activities and performance, permits the use of fewer rules and procedures, as
well as the delegation of decision-making authority. Control is apparently reduced, since
subordinates feel they have more decision-
making discretion, being responsible for more

decisions and subject to fewer formal rules
and procedures. This discretion, however, is
permitted because the consequences of their
activities can be assessed more completely and
more rapidly than without information technology. The evaluation system permits the organization to promote feelings of autonomy
while still having information to correct situations quickly.

CRITERIA FOR EVALUATION

In either outcome or process evaluation,
information is required. Further, in both instances, there are typically a multitude of
criteria available. For instance, sales persons could be evaluated on total sales, on the
number of repeat customers, on the number of
complaints, on the smoothness (lack of variation) in their sales rates, in the growth in
sales, in sales adjusted for some territorial
potential, and so forth. Since organizations
control incentives or resources valued by participants, evaluation is an explicit part of
the organizational process of control. In the
contest for resources and control that charac-
terizes organizations, the criteria and evaluation systems become an important concern.

In the typical management approach to this
topic, we are told that the manager, or group
of managers, decides what are the important
dimensions of organizational activity and performance, and then has the information system
designed to provide information on those prede-
fined important dimensions. But the typical
characterization of the process of information-
system design is misleading on two counts—
first, the criteria for evaluation are seldom
obvious, and are themselves an outcome of a
power struggle; second, the information system
as much determines what will be evaluated and
noticed as it reflects decisions about what
should be measured.

It is clear that persons or subunits will not
fare equally well regardless of what possible

criteria are chosen to evaluate them. Some
professors are excellent in research, others
are good instructors, others have administrative skills, and some have consulting capabilities. Some managers are better in dealing
with people, while others have analytical
strengths. Subunits also bring various competencies to the organization. Since there are
multiple criteria, and persons do not fare
equally well regardless of which are chosen,
there are contests concerning which criteria
are to be used in the evaluation. This struggle
over criteria is important because, depending
on what criteria are chosen, subunits and persons will be evaluated differently, and consequently will fare better or worse when resources are allocated in the organization. In
general, subunits will favor those criteria on
which they fare the best.

In a study of resource allocation at the
University of Illinois mentioned earlier,
Salancik and Pfeffer (1974) asked department
chairmen what the basis of the allocation of
the budget should be. Department chairmen were
also asked their relative positions on each of
the criteria, and objective data on several of
the variables were also obtained. Not surpris-
ingly, department chairmen tended to favor the
criteria on which they fared relatively better.
Departments with large undergraduate enrollments favored undergraduate enrollment as a
basis for budget allocation, while those with
high national rankings argued that national
prestige should be more important in allocating
budget.

Power, then, is used in determining what criteria of evaluation will be employed. Contests
over criteria are contests over control and influence. The dimensions of organizational activity that become stressed in the formal evaluation determine the character and behavior of
the organization. In the conflict over what the
organization should be doing and how the organization should be doing it, the evaluation
criteria provide the organization's answer, and

therefore evaluation systems become important
areas of conflict in organizations.

We should further note, however, that once in
place, information systems are not as precise
as our discussion may make them appear. There
is typically some room for maneuver in self-
presentation, manipulating and selectively
using information to enhance the evaluation of
oneself or one's subunit. There is, of course,
also some outright distortion or lying. In an
instance familiar to this author, a plant manager, unable to make his production quotas,
sent to headquarters false production output
reports. This continued until, in an inspection
of the warehouse, officials from the corporate
headquarters found practically no inventory,
instead of the large stock they expected to
find. However, such falsification of records
is not frequent. More frequent is the selective
reporting or the manipulation of information
to present oneself in the best possible light.
One method frequently employed is the selection
of a comparison standard. After all, few activities or performance measures make much sense
in isolation. They are relevant and useful only
when compared to something else. By choosing
comparison groups worse than the person being
evaluated, performance or activity can be made
to look better. Also, favorable parts of the
performance record can be stressed and less
favorable dimensions avoided. For a good lesson
in self-presentation and the selective use of
information, one might examine any experienced
executive's résumé.

Criteria, then, are used selectively, and
are the outcome of a contest of influence within the organization. Moreover, those things
that are measured receive attention, and those
that are not tend to be ignored in decision-
making. Ridgway (1956) has reviewed a number of
studies that indicate the effect of measurement, often unintended, on activity. His examples range from Soviet factories that, in
order to meet production goals "stormed" at the
end of the month, neglected maintenance to

Blau's (1955) description of a state employment service office, in which activity altered
as the measurement forms were changed. Information systems themselves provide data to organizational participants concerning what is
being assessed, and what, therefore, the organization must consider important. This information is used in deciding what activities
to engage in, and how much effort to devote to
each.

The information system itself comes to determine the criteria for evaluation. Those
things that are measured tend to be used,
particularly if they are easy to process, and
those that are not measured are not used in
the evaluation process. The admission criteria
to graduate school are an example of this effect. It has been shown (Gertler and Meltzer,
1970) that the Admission Test for Graduate
Study in Business (ATGSB) does not predict subsequent success, defined either in terms of
salaries for M.B.A.'s or number of publications
for doctoral students. The test, however, does
correlate with first-year graduate school
grades. In spite of the fact that the test does
not predict subsequent success, it is: (1) required by most schools and hence available,
and (2) easy to process, being a single number
that is even normalized to provide a percentile
distribution. As a consequence, this score is
used in deciding about admission to graduate
schools in business. A similar effect can be
observed in the issue of quantity versus quality of output. If quantity is measured, but
quality is not, perhaps because it is so much
more difficult to assess, the net effect is
that the quantity measures have large weight
in the evaluation process.

Because of the importance of the measurement
system in determining organizational behavior,
control over issues such as what should be
measured and how determines, in part, control
over the organization. Defining the dimensions
of the organization's information system is
tantamount to defining its system of

evaluation, which, in turn, provides control
and authority in the organization.

INFORMATION SYSTEMS AND POWER

We have already discussed how information
technology, through its enhancement of information-processing capabilities, can lead to a
centralization of control in organizations,
though the use of performance monitoring can
permit an increase in discretion and a reduction in formalization for many organizational
participants. Information technology, however,
is only one component of organizational information systems, and the effect just mentioned is only one of the ways that information and communication systems affect the distribution of influence in organizations.

Organizational information systems, particularly when they employ advanced information
technologies, provide enhanced processing capabilities and, equally important, a great deal
of information about organizational activities.
Consequently, it might be argued that the location of such information facilities in a given
subunit would enhance the power of that subunit
in the organization. Whisler (1970) did not
directly address this issue, but provided evidence that the location of the information
technology was perceived as an important decision by other organizational subunits. One
of the possible reasons for establishing a new
department, as so frequently occurs, is partially to overcome the interdepartmental rival-
ry that would prevent the computer system from
being effectively housed in an existing subunit such as production or accounting. Making
the analogy with the small group network experiments, there is likely to be a positive
relationship between centrality and influence
in the organization. The computer, because of
its importance in assessing and controlling

organizational performance, is likely to increase the centrality of any subunit where it
is housed. But the argument for the importance
of the information system, and centrality in
that system for establishing influence, is true
even when the system is not technologically
sophisticated. The department charged with
maintaining records and processing information
on organizational activities will always have
certain advantages in exercising influence.

This effect of information system centrality
on subunit power might tend to explain the importance of accountants and the power of financial officers and budget officials, not only in
corporations, but in governmental and other
nonprofit organizations. as well. To the extent,
however, that information collection and processing is kept dispersed throughout the other
subunits, there will not be a central informa-
tion-handling department or, in any event, it
will not have as much influence.

In the first chapter, we reviewed the strategic contingencies' theory of intraorganizational power, which held that power was related
to the ability to cope with critical organizational uncertainties. The link between this
theory and the importance of information systems and information technology in influencing
the distribution of control is direct. The reduction of uncertainty requires information.
Those in the organization who have control of or
access to critical information, which can be
used to reduce organizational uncertainties, acquire power because of their position. The strategic contingencies' theory also emphasized the
importance of substitutability in diminishing
subunit power. If other units in the organization have the same access to or control over
information, then none of them has a particular
advantage. In order to use information to reduce uncertainty and create power in the organization, one must have a monopoly on the information.

INFORMATION CONTROL AS A STRATEGY FOR OBTAINING POWER

The importance of control over information in achieving and maintaining influence in organizations seems almost self-evident. Nevertheless, we will provide some illustrations of the concepts we have been discussing.

In a study of decision-making concerning the selection of computing equipment, Pettigrew (1973, ch. 9) detailed strategies for power use, including the importance of information control and access. Pettigrew found that Kenny, the department head, was able to have his way over the opposition of two subordinates, through his position as the linking agent between his department, the outside computer manufacturers, and the board of directors. Pettigrew's analysis indicated clearly (1973, pp. 238-239) that Kenny used his position of access to the board to influence the decision, systematically biasing the information and presenting favorable and unfavorable comments to form impressions in such a way that the board would come to favor his own choice. Kenny also derived power from generalized access to board members because of his organizational role, as well as from his functioning as a technical gatekeeper. Access to and control of information enable organizational participants to filter information, manage information received by other organizational decision-makers, and in sum, effectively influence the decision process.

I have seen a similar situation in the case of the operation of university departments. I am frequently told that faculty govern the university, and particularly control the destiny of their own departments. Yet, interaction with higher level of administrators is typically channeled through a very few administrative positions. This gives the gatekeepers the ability to influence decisions. The summarization of information can be, and almost inevitably is, done in such a way as to reflect the biases

of the summarizer. It is possible to diffuse
responsibility for a decision through various
subunits, and thereby further to increase the
influence of those in the gatekeeping roles.
If a person is to be hired by one department,
then the department can discuss the issues and
make a decision. But if coordination with
another unit is involved, the department head,
who probably serves in the gatekeeping role,
can represent to the other department support
from his own department, and to his own department support from the other. This creates a
situation in which each department feels the
other strongly supports the case and goes
along, even though neither by itself might have
decided to hire the person.

Next, consider the importance of information
control for enhancing the power of top administrators, the authorities in the organization.
In the late 1960s, colleges and universities
confronted a major financial crisis. Funding
for both private and public universities became
increasingly scarce. In part as a response to
the scarcity of resources, and in part as a
continuation of an already existing trend to
more scientific and professional administration, many colleges and universities increased
administrative personnel as information systems
were developed and upgraded. Computer-based information systems that can provide information on enrollments in minute detail, as well as salary and
staffing data, are not uncommon on campuses. These
information systems, instituted to achieve the
economies of rational administration, have
tended to alter fundamentally the balance of
power in universities in favor of the administrators. Now, academic debates dealing with
values and priorities are overwhelmed by the
ability of administrators to produce reams of
figures on every aspect of the organization's
operations. The reality of the computer paper
customarily hides questions such as the validity or the usefulness of the numbers for an-
swering the questions being posed. Information,
particularly if on computer paper, takes on a

reality and importance independent of its con-
tent, as many students and corporate staff
members know as they prepare reports to impress
their teachers or supervisors. Moreover, it is
inevitably the case that the control of such a
data base provides those in control with dis-
tinct informational advantages in decision-making discussion and in their ability to analyze
and control organizational activities. Control
of a large data base on organizational operations, along with control of information channels, provides power.

We should note that the operation of information systems assumes a willingness on the part
of organizational members to comply—to furnish
the information and not to interfere with the
collection of information from others. Organized resistance to furnishing information is
infrequent in organizations, but there are instances of providing misleading or biased data,
particularly when one's job or position is at
risk. Because of the cooperation typically required to collect the information that is necessary for those in power to maintain and use
their power, it is useful for information collection to be justified in other terms besides
that of control or influence—such as increasing cost-effectiveness, or efficiency, or the
delivery of services. Indeed, management does
require information. But that does not invali-
date the fact that the maintenance of control
and influence also is facilitated through centralized information systems.

SECRECY AND THE DISTRIBUTION OF INFORMATION

Lasswell (1936) has asked the question who
gets what, but the question of who *knows* what
has not been examined. In every organization,
there is an unequal distribution of knowledge
about the organization's activities and structure. There may be varying degrees of ignorance
about salaries, criteria for evaluation, budgets, performance data, and staffing. Some of

the lack of knowledge may be self-imposed—after all, everyone is not interested in knowing everything about every aspect of an organization's operations. However, some of the differences in access to knowledge are intentional, and are strategically used by both authorities and various interest groups in their contest for organizational resources and control. Examination of the distribution of knowledge and information in an organization can provide valuable insights into the organization's structure of influence.

As Gamson noted, attempts to influence are more likely to be made when the organizational participants believe themselves to be affected by a decision, and when they believe they will not fare well unless they attempt to exert influence (1968, p. 145). Both these perceptions are, in part, dependent on the information the organizational members have. For instance, one method for keeping persons contented with their share of organizational resources or control is by making them believe that they are faring well with respect to others. In order to pursue such a strategy, however, it is necessary to keep information private that might be used to make social comparisons among persons or subunits.

Secrecy about pay is an example of how secrecy may be used in organizations. People develop notions of equitable pay through a process of social comparison (Smith, 1973, ch. 2), in which they evaluate their backgrounds, experience, job performance, and the pay received against the pay received and skills of others in the organization. If such information is not available because of pay secrecy, the employees must either evaluate the fairness of compensation by testing the job market, or rely on the organization to treat them fairly. Leventhal et al. (1972), in an experimental study, has indicated that subjects who make pay allocations that they know will be kept secret make more discrimination between high and low performers, producing a pay distribution with a

larger range. What Leventhal did not investi-
gate is, if you permitted the experimental subjects to keep that portion of the money not
allocated, whether they would attempt to use
pay secrecy to reduce the amount paid overall,
by paying only the minimum amount demanded by
persons to remain in the organization.

Organizational mythologies develop to legitimate secrecy. Thus, in the instance of pay
secrecy, one may be told that not knowing what
others make promotes a greater feeling of
equality and solidarity, avoiding competition
within the organization. Secrecy in evaluation
is typically justified on the basis that this
protects all involved and permits a more fair
and impartial evaluation. One must be careful
to separate rationalizations which have arisen
(or have been introduced) to defend the limitation of information in social structures from
the real purposes served.

In order to contend effectively for control
of resources, one clearly needs access to information. Without knowing budgets or their
allocation, evaluations, or the process by
which various policies are formulated, subunits
are effectively prevented from using whatever
power they might otherwise possess in the organization. The use of "national security" as a
policy to restrict the dissemination of information, and then taking advantage of others'
ignorance, has, unfortunately, its organizational counterparts.

Although some of the variance in the possession of information in organizations may be ac-
cidental, it is also likely that information
control is a technique practiced by authorities
to maintain and enhance their influence within
social structures. It seems logical that secrecy will be intentionally employed only when
the decisions are contested and opposed by
those with significant influence. If the decisions or procedures are universally accepted,
secrecy is not necessary. If none of the other
participants has enough influence to mount a
credible threat of opposition, secrecy is

probably not required. It is only when there
is opposition with some influence that secrecy
is likely to be practiced.

SUMMARY

We have examined in this chapter how information technology, and information systems more
generally, affects the design and structuring
of organizations. Information technology has
the paradoxical effect of permitting more centralized control through the enhancement of
information-processing capabilities, while
providing the appearance of decentralizing and
reducing the formalization in organizations.
We have argued that management by exception, or
the delegation of decision-making authority and
the reduction of rules because higher management can more rapidly and accurately monitor
performance, does not represent a fundamental
shift in the locus of influence in organizations. Information technology also has possible
effects on designs. On the one hand, the need
for a division of labor is reduced, while on
the other hand, information technology permits
more complex and differentiated structures to
be managed.
Evaluation systems and the criteria used for
evaluating performance are themselves outcomes
of a political process. Power is used to try to
implement those criteria which favor one's own
position. Once implemented, criteria provide
information to organizational participants
about important activities, and therefore come
to direct behavior. Measurement itself affects
behavior in organizations, even when the information system collecting the measurements
has not been consciously planned. Information
that is collected and easy to use is employed
in decision-making; information that is not
systematically collected or is more difficult
to use is less likely to be so employed, regardless, to some extent, of considerations of
its validity.

Finally, the distribution of influence in organizations is directly affected by the control of and access to information in the organization. The reduction of uncertainty, requiring information, is itself a source of power, as is the ability to filter and summarize information resulting from a central position in the organizational communication network. The distribution of information in the structure determines who knows what, and consequently, the likelihood of policies and decisions encountering opposition, and the ability of other organizational participants to undertake a serious challenge to present practices. Secrecy and the social distribution of knowledge in a structure, it is argued, are occasionally intentional strategic maneuvers in the contest for control and influence.

REFERENCES

Bavelas, Alex. "Communications Patterns in Task-Oriented Groups." *Journal of the Accoustical Society of America 22* (1950): 725-30.

Blau, Peter M. *The Dynamics of Bureaucracy.* Chicago: University of Chicago Press, 1955.

Burlingame, John F. "Information Technology and Decentralization." *Harvard Business Review 39* (1961): 121-26.

Child, John. "Predicting and Understanding Organizational Structure." *Administrative Science Quarterly 18* (1973): 168-85.

Gamson, William A. *Power and Discontent.* Homewood, Ill.: Dorsey Press, 1968.

Gertler, Judith M., and Meltzer, Allan H. "Selecting Creative Ph.D. Candidates for Admission." *Journal of Experimental Education 38* (1970): 15-18.

Hall, Richard H. *Organizations: Structure and Process.* Englewood Cliffs, N.J.: Prentice-Hall, 1972.

Hoos, Ida R. "When the Computer Takes Over the Office."
Harvard Business Review 38 (1960): 102-12.

Lasswell, Harold. *Politics: Who Gets What, When, How.*
New York: McGraw-Hill, 1936.

Lawrence, Paul, and Lorsch, Jay. *Organization and Environment.* Boston: Division of Research, Harvard Business School, 1967.

Leavitt, Harold J. "Some Effects of Certain Communication Patterns on Group Performance." *Journal of Abnormal and Social Psychology 46* (1951): 38-50.

Leavitt, Harold J., and Whisler, Thomas L. "Management
in the 1980s." *Harvard Business Review 36* (1958):
41-48.

Leventhal, Gerald S.; Michaels, James W.; and Sanford,
Charles. "Inequity and Interpersonal Conflict: Reward Allocations and Secrecy About Rewards as Methods
of Preventing Conflict." *Journal of Personality and
Social Psychology 23* (1972): 88-102.

Mackenzie, Kenneth D. *A Theory of Group Structures.*
London: Gordon and Breach, 1975.

Meyer, Marshall W. *Bureaucratic Structure and Authority.*
New York: Harper and Row, 1972.

Pettigrew, Andrew M. *The Politics of Organizational Decision-Making.* London: Tavistock, 1973.

Pfeffer, Jeffrey, and Leblebici, Huseyin. "Information
Technology and Organizational Structure." *Pacific
Sociological Review 20* (1977): 241-261.

Ridgway, V. F. "Dysfunctional Consequences of Performance Measurements." *Administrative Science Quarterly
1* (1956): 240-47.

Salancik, Gerald R., and Pfeffer, Jeffrey. "The Bases
and Use of Power in Organizational Decision-Making:
The Case of a University." *Administrative Science
Quarterly 19* (1974): 453-73.

Scott, W. R.; Dornbusch, S. M.; Busching, B. C.; and
Laing, J. D. "Organizational Evaluation and Authority."
Administrative Science Quarterly 12 (1967): 93-117.

Simon, Herbert A. "The Corporation: Will It Be Managed by Machines?" In *Management and the Corporation, 1985*, edited by M. L. Anshen and G. L. Bach, pp. 17-55. New York: McGraw-Hill, 1960.

Smith, Peter B. *Groups Within Organizations*. London: Harper and Row, 1973.

Thompson, James D. *Organizations in Action*. New York: McGraw-Hill, 1967.

Whisler, Thomas L. *Information Technology and Organizational Change*. Belmont, California: Wadsworth, 1970.

Whisler, T. L.; Meyer, H.; Baum, B. H.; and Sorensen, P. F., Jr. "Centralization of Organizational Control: An Empirical Study of Its Meaning and Measurement." *Journal of Business 40* (1967): 10-26.

Technology

As Child (1972) has described in his review
of the literature on organizational structures,
three classes of determinants or correlates of
organizational structures have been examined
in the literature: size, technology, and environment. We will consider the organization's
environment in the next two chapters, and technology now.

In the middle 1960s, technology came into
fashion as an explanatory variable in organizational research. Perrow (1967), in a paper we
shall discuss in more detail later in this
chapter, even argued that technology could be
the basic analytical structure on which to base
comparative analyses of organizations of all
types. It is fair to say that technology as a
variable to explain organizational structures
never quite fulfilled its potential. We would
argue that this was because technology, at
least initially, was not related in any systematic way to the issue of governance and control

in organizations, which, as we have repeatedly stated, is the central concern of organizational design and action.

DIMENSIONS AND DEFINITIONS

Before we look at the literature on technology and structure, and see what technology tells and does not tell about designing organizations, we must consider what technology is, and how it is measured. Technology may be considered as the processes that transform input into output in the organization. Recall that in the systems model of organizations (Katz and Kahn, 1966), the organization is viewed as a kind of black box, taking in input, transforming the input, and then disposing of the output, which may be either goods, services, or information. In this framework, technology is what occurs in the transformation process. Alternatively, technology may be viewed as the connections or relationships between actions and consequences, or outcomes. This represents only a slightly different way of again talking about transformations. The technology of instruction, for example, becomes the knowledge about the connections between various activities and desired outcomes. Technology, in this view, is not the activities as much as the conscious and intended use of activities, including those performed by equipment, to accomplish some end.

Technology could also be defined as the mechanisms or methods used for accomplishing organizational tasks. Whether we define technology as what occurs in the transformation process, as the connections between actions and consequences, or as the methods and mechanisms for accomplishing organizational tasks, it is clear that technology is more than the organization's machinery. Indeed, a close examination of these definitions may reveal that technology is the organization's activities. Anything that goes on in an organization can,

at some level, be related to the organization's
work and tasks, and therefore, can be considered part of the organization's technology.

We should note that many different technologies may be employed in a single organization. Scott et al. (1971) have persuasively
argued that one fault in thinking about organizations has been the tendency to consider
the organization as a whole, particularly an
undifferentiated whole. Thus, researchers
write about organizational structure and organizational technology as if there were uniformity within the organization. Of course,
there is not. The technology of the personnel
department may be quite different, no matter
what dimensions are used to describe it, from
the technology of the production department,
or the sales department, or an R. and D.
department. Technologies differ across organizational subunits.

Technologies also frequently differ within
subunits as well. Unless the subunits are created to contain only persons doing the same (or
similar) tasks with similar skills, there will
likely be a mix of tasks within the subunit,
each requiring a different technology. Further,
different technologies are used over time, as
knowledge and skill relevant to doing the
tasks change. Thus, in a corporate planning department, employees may use a variety of technologies and skills. Some of the personnel may
be using mathematical models, others the computer in simulations, and still others, technologies associated with survey research. At
the same time, the secretarial support staff
uses yet another technology in preparing reports, and in all cases, including the prepara-
tion of reports, technology has changed over
time, becoming increasingly machine-based and
capital-intensive.

That different technologies are associated
with different tasks and subunits, and that
such technologies change over time, make it
important to specify precisely what components
of the organization we are talking about when

we speak of the relationship between technology
and structure. Neither one is a concept that
applies in an undifferentiated fashion to the
whole organization.

DIMENSIONS

The definitions provided for the concept of
technology are broad, and perhaps the best way
to understand what is meant by the concept is
to look at how it has been made operational.
Unfortunately, like many concepts in organizational behavior, each researcher has a tendency
to make the concept operational in his own way,
but certain prominent operational versions of
the concept of technology do exist.
One of the first efforts to relate technology
to organizational structure was a study of
small manufacturing firms in England by
Woodward (1965). Woodward thought of technology
in terms of its technical complexity, arguing
that the critical dimension of technology was
the ability to predict results. Woodward's
scale of technology operationally measured the
length of the production run, running from
prototype production on a special-order basis
through small batch, large batch, and mass
production, with process production, such as
in an oil refinery, at the other end of the
scale. Woodward's scale corresponds, roughly,
to the time at which the technology was introduced, with small batch and single unit production being the oldest form, mass production
being newer, and continuous process production
being the newest of the technologies on the
scale.
Perrow (1967) described technology in terms
of two dimensions. The first involved whether
the task was repetitive, whether the organization was confronted, in other words, with
similar stimuli all the time. The second dimension dealt with the ability to analyze the
task. These two dimensions were presumed to
vary independently, so that organizations
could face either repetitive or novel tasks

that were either capable or incapable of analysis. Perrow's discussion of technology has occasionally been related to the dimension of routineness.

Hage and Aiken (1969) focused on the routineness of the technology in their attempt to explain structural variations. Routineness was measured by asking employees whether they did the same thing repeatedly on their jobs. Litwak (1961) had discussed a similar dimension, the uniformity or nonuniformity of the task. Hickson et al. (1969) argued that technology had three dimensions: an operations technology, a materials technology, and a knowledge technology. In their study, an attempt to replicate Woodward, they focused solely on operations technology. This was measured by a scale of work-flow integration, derived from a factor analysis of several subscales. Essentially, the measure was the degree of automation of the equipment. In their abbreviated replications of the original study (see, e.g., Hickson et al., 1974), the automation scale is the one typically employed. This scale, then, seems to be closely related to Woodward's original concept.

Harvey (1968) argued that technology should be measured in terms of its specificity and diffuseness, measured by noting the number of changes in product and production process over a ten-year period. Mohr (1971) measured technology by using three dimensions: (1) noise level, (2) task interdependence, and (3) manageability (uniformity, complexity, and analyzability). Mohr's third dimension is clearly related to Perrow's discussion of technology.

The dimension of predictability or certainty underlies many of the discussions of technology we have reviewed. Slowly, writers have developed the idea that technology influences structure through its effect on the possibility of and techniques for controlling behavior in the organization (e.g., Woodward, 1970). Routineness, analyzability, and the degree of automation all affect structure through their impact on organizational control. This emerging argument is consistent with the perspective we have pursued in this book, but it has not been explicitly and theoretically developed to any great degree. Most of the research using technology as a variable occurred in the period 1965-70. After the publication of Woodward's 1970 book, in which she argued for the control perspective and further documented the difficulties with measuring technology, the importance of this line of research for analyzing organizational structures diminished.

There are several problems with many of the technology-structure studies. One is that they use standard statistical techniques, many of which assume independence among the independent variables. But frequently there are contingent relationships among the independent variables, violating the assumption of independence required by the analyses. Second, additive effects are almost always assumed, though it is quite plausible that interactions among variables may be determining structures (see Pfeffer and Leblebici, 1973). Third, surrogate measures are employed for both technology and structure. Given an imperfect and partial measurement of both technology and structure, it is understandably difficult to find consistent relationships among the measures. Most important, frequently no logical necessity or causal argument links the processes of interest to any of the measured variables.

THE CHOICE OF TECHNOLOGY

Commonly, researchers relating technology to organizational structure have argued for a causal relationship between technology and structure—in other words, that the organization's technology is causally related to dimensions of the structure. In a review of this literature, Mohr (1971) concluded that the emphasis on technology, as conceptualized and measured, had not paid off in understanding structures. One problem with this line of inquiry has been the assumption that technology causes structure. In fact, technology is chosen.

It is evident that organizations choose their domains, the set of activities that they will engage in. The choice of a domain, a line of business, affects the technology that the organization will probably employ. If an organization decides to go into the business of education (like some subsidiaries of Bell and Howell), it is not likely to use process production, nor is it likely to use mass production. On the other hand, if an organization goes into the business of manufacturing motor vehicles, it is not likely to use prototype production. The choice of a domain, and a set of activities and tasks, tends to constrain the organization's technology, but the domain is still chosen.

Even more important, given a task, client population, and domain, the organization may still choose the technology it will employ. Perrow (1970) provided an example of two centers in which juvenile offenders were housed. In one, the task had been defined to be routine, and the structure was operated in a centralized and formalized fashion. In the other, the task was defined as being neither routine, repetitive, nor analyzable. In that organization, the extent of formalization was much lower, and the organization was much more flexible and less centralized. Other examples come quickly to mind. Although one may think that art requires creativity, and is certainly not a task that can be routinized, that is probably only because creativity and uniqueness are implict in one's definition of art. But engravings and lithographs are occasionally mass produced, or at least are turned out in large batches, while at other times the production is clearly closer to prototype.

Two points are relevant. First, the routineness of the task is not determined by the task itself, but rather by how the organization divides up the total work, and by how the organization defines the task for itself. In Perrow's example of juvenile delinquency centers, or in the case of prisons or mental health facilities or schools, whether the task is certain, repetitive, routine, or simple depends on how the work is defined and subdivided or perceived. Second, the choice of task itself, let alone how the task is defined, is under the organization's control through its choice of domain. Both of these points have been recognized by Child (1972), who noted that technological determinism may have failed in part because it did not take into account the *choice* component of domain and technology.

But as soon as we admit that technology and task are chosen, we are back to confronting the issue of the basis of the choice. One basis is certainly instrumental effectiveness or efficiency, or profit or some other rational criterion. However, other bases also exist. It may be that the definition of the task and the choice of technology are used to maintain control by authorities in the organization, or are used by various interests in their contest for control. This possibility is certainly worth considering.

THE STRUCTURAL CONSEQUENCES OF TECHNOLOGICAL CHOICE

One way of considering the bases for the choice of technology is to consider some of the consequences that logically follow the choice of varying technologies. It seems from casual observation that most organizations are continually striving to increase their degree of mechanization and automation. In hospitals, automated blood analyzers now perform laboratory tests, and computers frequently analyze medical histories. The production of most physical products has moved at least to mass production, and frequently to process production. Indeed, one company now boasts it runs an entire bread factory with only six employees. The automation of the tasks of middle management formed the focus for much of the discussion of the impact of computerization. But although the move to more automated technology is typically justified on the basis of efficiency, there are other considerations as well.

Mass production technology particularly leads to the possibility of routinizing jobs. What formerly may have been a craft job now is decomposed into component parts, and the individual job segments are allocated to a large number of persons, giving a single person little to do. The effects of routinization have been described by Hage and Aiken (1969), who found routine technology associated with more formalization, or the use of rules, and with a more centralized decision structure. Since routinization of tasks makes the individual worker much more readily replaceable, the individual has much less power in the organization. Consequently, he can claim less independence and control over what goes on in the organization, and finds himself subject to closer control through rules, with less access to organizational decisions. We argue that routinization, through its reduction in the power of those doing the routinized tasks, leads to an increase in the control of the authorities, or management, and a decrease in the autonomy and influence of the workers producing the organization's product.

If this is the case, then routinization serves the interests of higher management by facilitating a further centralization of power. This centralization may occur even in the case of process production. It is frequently the case that persons tending automated factories are not those who repair the equipment when it malfunctions. Computer operators do not repair the computer, nor do the programmers. Operators of computer-controlled machinery, or of heavy materials-handling or production equipment, are often in a similar position—an adjunct to the machine but not deriving power from their ability to repair it when it malfunctions. Indeed, repair is frequently contracted to the selling organization in the form of service contracts, or in guarantees that accompany the purchase or lease of the machine.

In addition, control of behavior is now partially accomplished by the technology itself. The machinery, rather than a supervisor, determines the pace of the work, and may even check up on the operator through automatic quality control and inspection as well as the keeping of production records. Blau and Scott (1962) noted that such impersonal mechanisms of control were desirable, since they decreased the visibility of interpersonal power relationships. Such a result is likely, because the machinery may appear to run out of the direct control of either the workers or the immediate supervisors, changing the relationship between them to one of facilitating rather than monitoring, a function that is now performed mechanically.

The routinization and automation of production makes possible finer degrees of control over behavior. As part of the process, jobs must be defined and analyzed in minute detail, to provide for timing and sequencing. Such job analyses may have as a by-product the development of more precise standards of performance, and the routinization of organizational activities probably means that activities become more well defined, and hence more controllable.

Routinization, through the subdivision of tasks and the increasing automation of the work place, also increases the independence of the organization from much of the labor pool. The replacement of men with machinery means that there are fewer persons to fight for control, fewer persons to strike, and fewer, or at least less powerful, persons to be replaced.

We suggest, therefore, that the choice of technology, measured according to its routineness, is a political choice. It is used to increase the control of the management, and is resisted by those organizational participants who perceive the loss of influence in the organization as a consequence. The process, as we have described it, has been most frequently analyzed with respect to the introduction of computers. Pettigrew (1973), for instance, described the resistance of stock-control clerks to the introduction of computers. As it turned out, the computers merely removed the routine parts of the job, leaving the stock clerks with a more important job than before, so they ultimately liked the change. The stories of middle management's resistance to computers are legion. But the process of contending over technology is more general.

We can consider professionalization as a part of this contest over control of work and tasks, and by extension, a contest over the locus and basis for control of behavior in social structures. One of the characteristics of the process of professionalization is the development of autonomy and self-regulation. This is accomplished through the mechanism of a professional association, which frequently serves to enforce professional standards of conduct, practices, and a code of ethics developed within the profession. Pfeffer (1974, p. 102) argued that the process of professionalization may serve the economic and social status interests of the members of the profession. Certainly, many occupational groups, including watchmakers, plumbers, real estate agents, insurance agents, and barbers, have attempted to obtain licensing powers to regulate and restrict entry into their occupations, and have developed many of the trappings of professions. Although the defining characteristic of a profession is, presumably, a specialized body of knowledge (Goode, 1957; Wilensky, 1964), the attainment of professional status may require the maintenance of apparent expertise through the development of a mythology of special competence, if not through the reality of specialized skills.

We argue that the conflict between

professionals and bureaucracies, which has been such a prominent theme in the literature (see, e.g., Hall, 1968; Scott, 1965), is merely a special case of the contest for control over resources and activities that is general within organizations. In this instance, the profession, as a collective unit, has asserted its independence from certain dimensions of control by the organizational hierarchy, maintaining that professionals can be controlled only by their peers (which has typically meant practically no control at all). The parallels with French and Raven's discussion of expert power (1968), and Crozier's (1964) discussion of the use of expertise to obtain power, are striking. In each instance, the occupational group seeks to maintain more independence from hierarchical control and to achieve more power in the social structure. In each instance, this power is claimed by virtue of having special skills or competence. In virtually each case, rituals and myths are developed to reinforce the claim to special competencies, which may include the use of special languages, uniforms, and the development of a collective identity through associations.

The processes we have described are general. Computer programmers, systems analysts, operations researchers, marketing researchers, accountants, and engineers are only a few of the occupations within bureaucracies that have attempted to professionalize and achieve independence and power in their respective organizations through the symbolic use of their expertise. It is obvious that routinization and automation of tasks is antithetical to the aims of this professionalizing process, and thus will be resisted. Interestingly, the possession of specialized, critical skills is not an objective reality, but is created in part in this contest between participants and the authorities. The social definition of specialized skills becomes an arena for conflict, as each side seeks a definition of social reality that will enhance its relative power.

TECHNOLOGY AND EXTERNAL CONTROL

The choice of technology affects not only the distribution of power within the organization, but also the relationship between the organization and elements of its environment that seek to control its behavior. That is because technology may necessitate buffering the organization from its environment. Buffering, or the assurance of smooth demands on the organization, is most necessary when a process-production technology is employed, and is probably least necessary in the case of small batch production. Technologies differ not only in terms of their degree of automation, but also in whether they are general purpose or whether they are limited to the production of one product or a very narrow range of products. Clearly, the specificity of the technology affects the relationships between the organization and its environment.

In the case of general, multipurpose technologies, such as the general machining equipment in a small machine shop, the necessity of ensuring future demand for the same products is reduced. The organization possesses a technology which is flexible enough to make a variety of products for a variety of uses, and hence is more adaptable to the shifts in demand. Conversely, a special purpose, mass production, or process technology has much less flexibility. Changing from the production of small to large cars or vice versa requires a tooling expense of millions of dollars. Indeed, the ability of American Motors and Chrysler to respond to changes in market demand has been limited by their inability to undertake the type of retooling and redesign that might be desirable. A large oil refinery can change the mix between types of petroleum products, moving from heating oil to jet fuel to gasoline, but it cannot process soybeans, milk, or bread, or manufacture automobiles. Specialized technology, then, requires more buffering from environmental fluctuations, since the

technology itself cannot respond to changes
in demand.

Several consequences follow from this line
of argument. First, the development of specialized subunits to insulate the organization
from its environment or to manage that environment is more likely in the case of specialized
technologies. The general purpose machine shop
can quickly change from one product to another.
Given its potential adaptability, it requires
less insulation from changes in environmental
demand. On the other hand, specialized technology, which is not easily shifted from one
type of production or product to another, requires a steady demand for the same product.
One might predict, therefore, the greater prev-
alence of activities undertaken to ensure
steady and continuing product demand, such as
marketing, public relations, and lobbying in
industries employing specialized technologies.
This should be reflected in the number of buffering and boundary-spanning units that a
typical firm in such industries possesses.

Second, it is likely that subunits which link
the organization to its environment have relatively more power in the organization when the
organization-environment relationship is more
critical. In the case of process production,
once the plant is in operation, the production
process is largely routinized and predictable.
The ability to dispose of the output from the
production process, or the ability to acquire
the input material needed in the process, remains critical. This suggests that in the case
of specialized technologies, boundary-spanning
units will have more power, while in organizations employing more general-purpose technologies, the production and engineering departments will have relatively more influence.

The choice of technology, then, affects the
organization's potential adaptability to
changing environmental demands. When technology
is specialized, there will be more boundary-
spanning units and activities, and such units
will have relatively more power.

The choice of technology also affects the
organization's competitive relationships. While
routinization of tasks makes control of behavior within the organization easier, it also increases the possibility of competition. Since
specialized skills are not needed, there is no
difficulty in competing because of the un-
availability of labor. Further, since the task
has been divided into small, component parts,
the resulting product or service must necessarily be easily duplicated. Organizations must
trade off, then, between routinizing the task
and increasing internal control, and leaving
the organization's work less routinized--making
it more difficult for competitors to duplicate
exactly the organization's output.

The difference is illustrated if one listens
to an encyclopedia salesperson and a good real
estate agent. The encyclopedia sales presentation is routinized—a standard set of opening
remarks, questions and answers, and a standard
presentation. Indeed, the presentation is so
standard that one can recognize the approach
even before the salesperson tells you he is
selling encyclopedias. This routinized task
gives the seller little power. They are typically paid poorly, exploited, have little to
say in the company, and are easily replaced.
On the other hand, a good salesperson, say, for
real estate, does not have a standard presentation, but rather engages in a nonroutine activity which is modified through luck and experience to fit the situation. Such a person has
great power in the organization because his
skills are not easily replaced. The encyclopedia salespeople have less influence and are
easier to control, and it is also easier for a
competitor to copy their approach. The same expertise that gives a person influence who is
performing a nonroutine task makes it more difficult for a competing organization to duplicate the given organization's performance.

Finally, we can consider the use of technology in the relationships between the organization and its customers and suppliers. The

development of automated or complex technologies may provide the organization with influence with respect to external organizations.
Using competitors as the justification, the organization may keep its technology and production process secret from its customers. The development of a technological mystique makes the
customers believe that the organization they
are dealing with has some particular competence, and hence they are likely to be loyal
to the organization. A complex, elaborated
technology may similarly impress the customer.

A friend worked as a secretary for a legal
firm. Legal work is considered to be a highly
nonroutine task, requiring skill and competence;. yet our friend reported that she typed
wills using a standard format, inserting names
and specifics where appropriate. For a few
minutes' work, the lawyers were able to collect
enough information to give our friend (making
a relatively nominal wage) the job to be completed. This routine task was made to appear
nonroutine, first by keeping the existence of
such standardized forms secret, and second by a
series of activities designed to lead the client to believe the task to be indeed complex
and nonroutine. Such examples occur frequently
in organizations. The best situation is where
the task is routinized, so that participants
have relatively little influence, but the external world, both competitors and customers,
believes the task to be complex and nonroutine,
so the organization has influence with respect
to them as well.

We have developed a theme that appears frequently in this book: the meaning of action is
constructed, and the construction of meaning
is strategically used in the contest for control. The routineness or nonroutineness of the
technology is determined both by decisions
taken by the organization and by the perception
of the decisions concerning the choice of technology shared by observers. If everyone believes turning three bolts is a nonroutine
task, then for purposes of explaining relative

power and influence, it is. One is tempted to develop hypotheses concerning the place at which work is done, and the accessibility to scrutiny of the organization's task. One might argue that industrial secrecy is focused not only at competitors, but at customers as well. When the organization operates out of the view of the customers, it enhances the possibility of convincing them of the complexity and skill required to accomplish the job.

TECHNOLOGICAL CHANGE

The customary view of organizations has been that decentralized, less formalized structures facilitate rapid technological change or innovation (Hage and Aiken, 1970). Yet another view has been that rapid technological change itself causes less formalized, decentralized organizational structures. The question is whether structure causes innovation and change, or whether innovation and change, presumably caused by competitive pressures or other environmental factors, cause structure. A third alternative is that they cause each other, though one-way causality is what we typically find in the literature.

We would argue that neither question is particularly useful, asked in its usual terms. Innovation, technology, or change cannot be analyzed without considering the impact of the specific change on the distribution of influence in the organization, a point we will pursue in greater detail in chapter 7. Our purpose here is to note that if technology is chosen, and chosen using considerations of control as well as efficiency, then it is likely that technology can best be viewed as an outcome, rather than as a cause, of fundamental organizational processes. The choice of technology and the organizational design both reflect and affect the distribution of control in the organization. Each is caused by the contest for control in the organization, and the resources that are brought to bear in this contest. The fact that the two variables, technology and structure, occasionally vary together depends more on the strategy of the political contest than on determinate relationships derived from considerations of organizational efficiency.

REFERENCES

Blau, Peter M., and Scott, W. Richard. *Formal Organizations*. San Francisco: Chandler, 1962.

Child, John. "Organizational Structure, Environment and Performance: The Role of Strategic Choice." *Sociology 6* (1972): 2-22.

Crozier, Michel. *The Bureaucratic Phenomenon*. Chicago: University of Chicago Press, 1964.

French, John R. P., Jr., and Raven, Bertram. "The Bases of Social Power." In *Group Dynamics*, edited by Darwin Cartwright and Alvin Zander, pp. 259-69. New York: Harper and Row, 1968.

Goode, W. "Community Within a Community: The Professions." *American Sociological Review 22* (1957): 194-200.

Hage, Jerald, and Aiken, Micahel. "Routine Technology, Social Structure and Organizational Goals." *Administrative Science Quarterly 14* (1969): 366-77.

_____. *Social Change in Complex Organizations*. New York: Random House, 1970.

Hall, Richard H. "Professionalization and Bureaucratization." *American Sociological Review 33* (1968): 92-104.

Harvey, Edward. "Technology and the Structure of Organizations." *American Sociological Review 33* (1968): 247-59.

Hickson, David J.; Pugh, D. S.; and Pheysey, Diana C. "Operations Technology and Organization Structure: A Reappraisal." *Administrative Science Quarterly 14* (1969): 378-97.

Hickson, David J.; Hinings, R.; McMillan, C. J.; and Schwitter, J. P. "The Culture-Free Context of Organization Structure: A Tri-National Comparison." *Sociology 8* (1974): 59-80.

Katz, Daniel, and Kahn, Robert L. *The Social Psychology of Organizations*. New York: John Wiley, 1966.

Litwak, Eugene. "Models of Bureaucracy Which Permit Conflict." *American Journal of Sociology 67* (1961): 177-84.

Mohr, Lawrence B. "Organizational Technology and Organizational Structure." *Administrative Science Quarterly 16* (1971): 444-59.

Perrow, Charles. "A Framework for the Comparative Analysis of Organizations." *American Sociological Review 32* (1967): 194-208.

Pettigrew, Andrew M. *The Politics of Organizational Decision-Making*. London: Tavistock, 1973.

Pfeffer, Jeffrey. "Some Evidence on Occupational Licensing and Occupational Incomes." *Social Forces 53* (1974): 102-11.

Pfeffer, Jeffrey, and Leblebici, Huseyin. "The Effect of Competition on Some Dimensions of Organizational Structure." *Social Forces 52* (1973): 268-79.

Scott, W. R. "Reactions to Supervision in a Heteronomous Professional Organization." *Administrative Science Quarterly 10* (1965): 65-81.

Scott, W. R.: Dornbusch, S. M.; Sagatun, I.; Evashwick, C. J.; and Magnani, L. "Task Conceptions and Work Arrangements." Paper presented at the 66th Annual Meetings of the American Sociological Association, Denver, Colorado, August 30, 1971.

Wilensky, Harold L. "The Professionalization of Everyone?" *American Journal of Sociology 70* (1964): 137-58.

Woodward, Joan. *Industrial Organization: Theory and Practice*. London: Oxford University Press, 1965.

_____. *Industrial Organization: Behaviour and Control*. London: Oxford University Press, 1970.

5

The Organizational Environment

If organizations have any goal generally agreed upon by all participants, it is survival. Survival for an organization, an open social system, requires the maintenance of favorable exchange relationships with other groups and organizations in the environment. This frequently involves producing some good or service desired by the market. These other organizations with which the focal organization exchanges are also interested in the organization's activities. They have a stake in the organization's decisions, as they are interdependent with it. There is, then, not only a contest for control over organizational behavior waged within the organization's boundaries, but external groups as well may attempt to influence organizational actions and policies. The necessity of transacting with outside groups means that those in the organization who cope with this interdependence acquire more influence, particularly to the extent that such interdependence becomes problematic.

Organizational structures are designed to cope with external interdependence, including competitive interdependence. Further, such structures must be able to deal with the uncertainty and changing patterns of tastes, norms, and values confronted by the organization. Interdependence with external organizations affects the influence of internal subunits, which is also likely to be reflected in the resultant organizational structures. In this chapter, we continue our exploration of variables affecting organizational design by examining some of the effects of the organization's environment.

ORGANIZATIONAL SURVIVAL AND GROWTH

In an organization, it is reasonable to argue that all parties in or transacting with the organization have an interest in seeing it survive. While there may be, and probably are, differences in how participants believe resources should be allocated or in objectives, each party who is a member of, or transacting with, the organization is interested in the organization's survival. Assuming relatively free movement of persons among organizations, and assuming the ability to engage freely in exchanges among organizations, one can argue that membership or other participation with an organization is a choice which indicates that the group involved can gain more from this activity than from alternatives, subject to the constraints of limited search and information, of course. Thibaut and Kelley (1959), in an analogous fashion, have noted that for an interaction to be maintained, the outcomes received by the participants must be better than the outcomes perceived to be available from alternate interaction arrangements. So,

in organizations participants are most likely
receiving something that is better than they
could obtain in other organizations, and hence
they have an interest in the organization's
continuation.

Not only is survival a generally agreed-upon
objective, but so is the growth of the organization. Organizational growth increases the
likelihood of the organization's survival.
Large organizations are not permitted to go
out of existence like small organizations. They
have constituencies and an impact that provides them, because of their size, with claims
on society's resources necessary for their
continuation. While small, "mom and pop" retail stores open and close continually, large
organizations, such as Lockheed, are kept operating even with extraordinary measures.
This is because the failure of a small organization has limited impact, but the failure or
closing of a large organization has greater
impact, and therefore is more likely to be
prevented by political intervention.

In addition to increasing the organization's
capacity for survival, growth provides two
other advantages. First, growth usually means
that there are more resources to be divided
among the participants. More resources mean
that instead of as much conflict over the
division of resources, all participants can
get more out of a steadily increasing pool of
resources. Conflict is less likely under conditions of constant organizational expansion.
As long as participants are getting more,
their relative shares are a less salient issue. When organizational growth stops, or organizational contraction begins, conflict
among participants over the share of the resources increases. Since conflict is typically
not pleasant, and organizational growth avoids,
to some extent, conflict among participants,
organizational growth is favored. A colleague
tells of a discussion with a famous professor
at a university about the allocation of resources to various specialties within a

department. The professor noted that when resources were plentiful and increasing, his colleagues could tell him that allocations to the
other specialties had no effect on his share—
his group could get what they could reasonably
expect in any event. With resources now scarce,
this was no longer the case, and fighting among
the groups in the department had increased. This
phenomenon is consistent with the hypothesis
that the use of power will increase under conditions of increasing resource scarcity
(Salancik and Pfeffer, 1974).

Organizational growth also provides the organization with more power with respect to
other organizations and groups in its environment. In the next chapter we will discuss some
possible methods organizations employ in attempts to control their environments. Organizations have advantages in these efforts to
the extent that they have more resources. Size
provides some measure of power, other things
being equal, in a system of organizations.
This power, of course, can be used to extract
more resources from the environment, to be
shared among participants, and to further organizational growth and survival.

REQUIREMENTS FOR SURVIVAL

Katz and Kahn (1966) have described organizations as open systems, and elaborated the
consequences of this view in some detail.
Briefly, organizations engage in a cycle in
which they acquire input, such as capital, raw
materials, and labor, produce some set of
goods and services, and then deliver these
goods or services back into the environment.
The cycle of resource acquisition, transformation, and output means that the organization
must depend on other groups and organizations
both in the input-acquisition and in the out-
put-disposal phase of the cycle.

Organizations require input of personnel and
financial resources in order to continue in
existence. Even noneconomic organizations,
such as churches, schools, and political

parties, must recruit and compensate some personnel, pay rent, and use other resources that
must be paid for. But financial resources and
personnel are not all that organizations require. In order to be able to attract and retain the resources needed to survive, organizations require at least some measure of social legitimacy.

Organizational legitimacy is a concept that
has been written about frequently but studied
only infrequently. Legitimacy may be relevant
to the organization's product, its method of
production, or to the organization as a whole.
Thus, an organization may produce a legitimate
product, such as food, through an illegitimate
production process, such as the use of forced
labor. Or, an organization may employ and pay
persons legitimately to produce an illegitimate
product, such as pollution or napalm. Legitimacy is determined by the social consensus, the
social value judgments applied collectively to
the organization. Although clearly not all
groups or individuals are likely to perceive
organizational products or processes similarly,
to the extent that a social consensus exists,
legitimacy or illegitimacy is defined by that
consensus.

Dowling and Pfeffer (1975) noted that the
concepts of legitimacy, legality, and economic
viability were not identical. The law tends
to be more internally consistent than social
values and to lag behind changes in norms.
Economic viability is dependent on many factors. Products may be in demand but not legitimate, such as narcotics, or not be economically
viable in a market mechanism, but legitimate.
Legitimacy is important because of the position
of organizational claims to societal resources.
In order for organizations to be able to acquire and use inputs, the use of such inputs
by the organization must be perceived as socially legitimate. Otherwise, society, through
its organizational agents, will act to prevent
the organization's acquisition of inputs that
may be required for its survival. Legitimacy,

like other organizational inputs, is acquired
from the environment.

Organizations frequently obtain the resources to continue the cycle of input acquisition and production through the selling of
the organizational output in some form of
market. The clients or customers of the organization, through their purchase of the organization's product, provide the money required for the organization to pay personnel
and obtain other inputs. However, the organization's ability to acquire resources and obtain more inputs is not always directly contingent on the organization's sale of some
product or service to some customer or clients.
Prisons, mental institutions, and welfare departments are three social service agencies
in which the clients being served have no ability to go to alternative organizations and no
resources that the organizations require. Consequently, there is no requirement for the organizations involved to serve these clients in
order to ensure a continued supply of resources. Alternatively, business firms must
sell a product or service in order to obtain
the resources necessary to continue in existence. Although firms may operate in markets
in which there are more or fewer competitors,
the customers or clients must still engage in
transactions voluntarily, and are able to withhold their resources from organizations they
do not feel are providing for their demands.

It is possible, of course, to argue that the
prisons, mental institutions, and welfare offices also provide services for their clients,
but that the clients are other groups and political organizations in the society. Thus,
prisons provide security, or at least a sense
of security, for the persons not incarcerated;
welfare organizations provide vehicles for
which persons with income can provide charity
and support to the deserving poor. The importance of the linking or nonlinking of resources with various client groups cannot be
overstated. It is likely that organizations,

seeking to survive, will produce those products or services desired by those with the ability to pay and those directly sponsoring and funding the organization. The related idea, that organizations will respond to an interest group to the extent it has direct control over resources needed by the organization, has led to innovations such as the use of educational vouchers in school systems, and other similar experiments to reintroduce competition and provide those served by the organization with the power to give or withhold resources that the organization needs.

RESOURCE INTERDEPENDENCE AND THE CONTROL OF ORGANIZATIONS

Because organizations require resources in order to survive, and because growth is often another organizational objective also requiring resources, the process of resource acquisition is an important focus of organization attention. Since organizations, as open social systems, are inevitably not self-contained, and require transactions with other, external organizations, then relationships of interdependence develop with those external organizations.

There is interdependence between the interacting organizations because each depends on the other. The small supplier selling to General Motors needs the sales in order to continue in business, while at the same time General Motors uses the supplies purchased as input to its production process. Although exchange relationships invariably involve some degree of interdependence among the organizations, we can break the transaction in half, and ask about each organization's dependence on the other. The relationship between dependence and power is direct, and has been commented on and developed by several authors. Emerson (1962) noted that power was the result of dependence relations, a position argued by Blau (1964) as

well. Emerson's initial formulation stated that
the power of b over a (which was the same as
a's dependence on b) was a function of: (1)
the importance of the resources or outcomes
that b controlled to a, and (2) the availability of the resources, actions, or outcomes
from other actors. Dependence, therefore, was
a consequence of the importance of an outcome
to a social actor and the control of the other
party over that outcome.

Blau (1964) argued that power differences
among actors inevitably occurred in exchange
relationships. However, Blau further hypothesized that such power differences were not
completely stable, since the less powerful
party would make various attempts to reduce
the power of the other over it, by devaluing of
the resource or outcome received from the relationship, developing alternative sources, or
using force to obtain the performance or outcome of the other party.

In a study of resource allocation in a university (Pfeffer and Salancik, 1974), we had
occasion to interview the head of a particular,
less powerful department. In the course of the
interview, he emphasized over and over the
graduate orientation of the department and how
important the graduate program was. We were,
therefore, quite surprised to find that he
rated the importance of university-provided
graduate fellowships as fairly low. He told
us that since he did not get any of these,
he had developed alternative sources of support for his graduate students. Therefore, such
fellowships were now not critical. We also suggest that had he not been able to find alternative support, then the importance of graduate education would have been reduced. This
exemplifies the type of adjustment Blau was
referring to.

Jacobs (1974) has extended the propositions
of Emerson to consider power relationships
among formal organizations. And Pfeffer (1972)
has added two other variables to the consideration of the development and use of power based

on dependent relationships among organizations. Defining dependence in a fashion analogous to that of Emerson, Pfeffer noted that in addition to dependence, in order to observe behavioral control of one social actor over another, there must also be: (1) the ability to use the dependence to effect control, and (2) some discretion in the behavior of the party to be controlled. There are many instances in which legal proscriptions, for example, make the use of a dependence relationship to effect control of behavior impossible. The antitrust laws are full of such instances. So, a large supplier cannot use its position of dominance to force the smaller distributor to sell out, or to control the sales price or territory of the distributor.

The ability to use the dependence is also limited when the resources are controlled by someone who is no longer alive. Universities, hospitals, and other organizations that receive charitable contributions undoubtedly prefer such "dead money," or money that comes to it through bequests. Once such money has passed, there is no way for the person to use these resources to attempt to influence the actions of the receiving organization.

In order for dependence to be used to control the actions of another organization, the organization in question must have the discretion to alter its actions. The organization may lack such discretion because of legal restrictions, or because it is already constrained by other organizations on which it is as, or even more dependent. Student demonstrations over tuition at many state universities will do no good if focused at the university or campus administration. Tuition decisions may be made at the level of the regents, or perhaps by the legislature itself. Thus, attempts to influence would be more effective if focused on those who control the actions of the organization in question, rather than on the organization itself. Indeed, groups learn this; now students in many states have their

own lobbyists to present their side of issues
to the state legislators. Organizations frequently attempt to resist altering actions by
claiming that other organizations or groups
would not permit the change. The intentional
cultivation of such pressure to oppose pressure
from other organizations has occasionally been
undertaken. Thus, dependence is not sufficient
to ensure control of behavior. The dependence
must be usable, according to legal and normative systems, and the organization being influ-
enced must have discretionary control over the
action or outcome in question.

SOCIAL CONTROL OF ORGANIZATIONS

The social control of individuals in a society has long been a topic of interest, but
recently people have begun to pay attention to
the use of interdependence and interorganizational power in the social control of organizations in society.

One of the mechanisms of social control is
the accrediting organization. Wiley and Zald
(1968) examined the growth and transformation
of two educational accrediting organizations.
Attention recently has also been paid to the
activities of the Joint Commission on the Accreditation of Hospitals (JCAH) and its role
in the control of hospitals. Accrediting organizations have influence on the organizations
they accredit only to the extent that accreditation is important in affecting the flow of
other resources to the organization. Thus, accrediting of educational organizations is critical to the extent that flows of students,
contributions, grants, and contracts are affected. The accrediting organization itself
faces a dilemma, caused by its own interdependence. If it accredits all organizations,
or almost all, the accreditation itself does
not discriminate among organizations, and consequently, has little value. On the other hand,
if the organization accredits too few, those

unaccredited organizations may establish or
support a competing accrediting agency.

In actual operation, accrediting organizations are frequently constrained in their effects by the fact that their own resources
come from fees received from accredited organizations, or members of the accrediting association. Furthermore, in many instances, resources
do not follow accreditation, giving the fact of
accreditation little significance for organizational growth and survival. Such is certainly
the case with the JCAH and with many educational accrediting organizations. The accreditation itself has low salience, and does not
directly affect flows of resources.

Contrast this with the situation of the
National Collegiate Athletic Association
(NCAA). Through its arrangements with post-
season tournaments and bowl games and with the
television networks, NCAA penalties do have
resource consequences for the organizations involved. The television revenues a school receives, as well as its national exposure, are
important in its athletic programs. As a consequence, the NCAA potentially has greater
control over its member organizations. However,
even in this instance, the affected organizations have countervailing power. Since viola-
tions of regulations are widespread (some might
say almost universal), the NCAA faces a quan-
dary. If it enforces all of its regulations
strictly, there would be too many affected organizations, who might withdraw and make independent arrangements with the bowls and television networks, who after all are primarily
interested in revenues as well. Consequently,
the NCAA follows the practice of punishing only
those organizations who are reported, and the
pattern of punishments tends to be one in which
the severity of penalties is biased against
smaller, less powerful schools (Stern and
Reynolds, 1974).

The important point is that because of interdependence with external organizations, this
interdependence, and the requirement for

resources can be used by organizations of
social control to influence the activity of organizations in the society. However, these organizations have themselves requirements
for resources and survival, which means that
in operation is a system of exchange and mutual
control.

POWER OF INTERNAL SUBUNITS

Since organizations need to acquire inputs
and engage in successful exchanges with other
organizations in their environments in order
to survive, one basis of power in the organization is a subunit's ability to facilitate the
process of resource acquisition or to manage
external interdependence. Those interdependencies that are the most problematic, or those
resources that are the most critical, are more
important contingencies for the organization,
thereby providing the subunits that cope with them
relatively more influence in the organization.
This is one reason why boundary-spanning positions in organizational structures are frequently influential.

As noted previously, the capability of ensuring continued support by an external organization requires that the focal organization
make some commitments of its own. Alliances
between internal and external organizational
participants are quite possible, in each instance serving to enhance the interests of each
without necessarily serving the interests of
the total organization. Thompson (1962), in his
discussion of output transactions, a particular
boundary relationship, noted that organizations
sought to impose rules governing transactions,
to avoid the possibility that, say, a purchasing agent would use his position to extract resources for himself. It is certainly easy to
see the forces that would lead to the development of stable relationships among persons in
reciprocal boundary-spanning positions. The
purchasing agents want to ensure a reliable
source of supply, and the salesperson wants to

sell the product. It is in the interests of each to stabilize their interactions and reduce uncertainty for each, a relationship that may be cemented by an exchange of various gifts or favors.

In another context, Hunt and Hunt (1971) noted the stability of the relationships between the Department of Defense and the National Aeronautics and Space Administration and their principal contractors. To reduce uncertainty and manage external interdependencies, it is likely that organizations seek to stabilize relationships with other important organizations in their environments. Those in the organization responsible for this task acquire power to the extent that such relationships are both problematic and critical for the organization.

INTERDEPENDENCE AND STRUCTURE

One response to organizational interdependence is an attempt to manage or negotiate the interdependence, a topic we will discuss in more detail in the next chapter. However, some authors have argued that interdependence and dependence have consequences for the design of organizational structures. These structural consequences of interdependence we will consider now.

Aiken and Hage (1968) argued that resource limitations caused social service agencies to undertake joint programs with other agencies. These joint programs created interdependence among the agencies, and the observed structural correlates of such interdependence included greater structural complexity, more professional staff, and less formalization. That the study was carried out on 16 health and welfare organizations possibly limits the ability to generalize about it, and it is uncertain whether the joint programs caused the interdependence, as Aiken and Hage argued, or whether

the joint programs were themselves responses
to interdependence.

The most comprehensive examination of the
effect of dependence on organizational structure was that undertaken by the Aston group in
England. Dependence was thought of as including
relations with a parent organization and relations with other organizations (Pugh et al.,
1969). Dependence on the parent organization
was measured using four scales: (1) relative
size of the organization compared to the
parent, (2) legal status of the subsidiary,
(3) representation of focal organization in
decision-making bodies of the parent, and (4)
number of specializations contracted outside
of the focal organization. Dependence on other
organizations was assessed using a scale measuring vertical integration, and two other
measures, one assessing the public accountability of the parent organization, and the other
the impersonality of origin of the focal organization. The various components of dependence were in turn factor analyzed, producing
a main factor labeled dependence (Pugh et al.,
1969, p. 108). This dependence measure was
correlated with the concentration of authority
($R = 0.66$), but not with the other two measures
of structure used by the Aston group, the
amount of structuring of activities and line
control of the work flow (Pugh et al., 1969,
p. 107). The principal finding, then, of the
Aston research and its replications (see, e.g.,
Inkson et al., 1970) is the effect of dependence on increasing centralization in the organization.

Mindlin and Aldrich (1975) have criticized
the Aston results, particularly for the con-
founding of dependence on a parent organization
with dependence on the environment more generally. An attempt by these authors to analyze
the Aston data was not outstandingly successful, because of the limitations inherent in the
data set and the sample size. However, in the
literature that exists conflicts arose over the

effect of interdependence, or dependence, on
the centralization of organizations. Aiken and
Hage (1968) developed a model that would essentially predict that dependence would lead
to decentralization, less formalization, and
increased professionalization of the work
force, while Pugh et al. (1969) have argued the
reverse effect, particularly for centralization.

Recall that by Emerson's (1962) formulation,
dependence was the converse of power. Since the
Aston measures of dependence focused primarily
on the relationship between the focal organization and its parent, it is scarcely surprising
that they found a negative relationship between
dependence and autonomy from the parent organization. It seems that the critical question for
assessing the structural consequence of dependence is where in the organization the capability for dealing with the dependence resides.
Other things being equal, central authorities
are likely to argue that dependence on an external organization requires centralized, top-
management concern. Certainly, for example, as
universities have become more dependent, and
the dependence more problematical, attempts
have been made to control information flowing
from within the organization to the outside,
and to centralize the task of coping with the
dependence relationships. However, the ability
to centralize control when confronted by dependence rests on the ability of the central
authorities to cope with the dependence. If,
for instance, dependence-coping requires the
skills of other organizational participants,
then decentralization will result. In most
instances, we would argue, the institutional
relationships among organizations are handled
at the top of the organization. Therefore, in
most instances, dependence is likely to lead to
increased control over lower level participants, and participants who are involved in
boundary transactions. However, such control,
accomplished through either formalized rules
or centralized decision-making, or some

combination of both, will not be observed when these other participants control the critical contingencies, information, and resources necessary to cope effectively with the dependence relationships. In this case, new units or activities will probably be established to work on task routinization, facilitating efforts to recentralize control.

THE EFFECTS OF COMPETITION

One specific form of interdependence among organizations is competitive interdependence. In a study of 37 small manufacturing organizations, Pfeffer and Leblebici (1973) argued that competition represented increased external pressure on the organization, and that the response to such external pressure would be an increase in control within the organization. Korten (1962) argued that war typically has resulted in a centralization of decision-making within nations. Lawrence and Lorsch (1969, p. 26) argued that competition is a form of pressure that may lead to increased demands for control within the organization. The opposite argument is that competition represents uncertainty, and that in order to cope with uncertainty, decentralized structures are required, a point to be examined in more detail below. Also, it might be argued that competition requires flexibility and speed of response. Here the structural implications are contradictory. On the one hand, it might be argued that centralized structures, through a simplified control system and concentration of authority, permit more rapid response to environmental changes. On the other hand, Thompson (1967, ch. 6) has argued that centralized decision-making may lead to less adaptability. The critical intervening variable is whether or not the capacity of the centralized structure is sufficient. Clearly, if decisions are all made at one or two organizational positions, and these positions become overburdened

with information, responsiveness will diminish.
On the other hand, if the positions are not
overburdened, unified and coordinated change
will be achieved more rapidly than if decision-
making authority is widely dispersed, requiring
consultation and coordination among a large
number of persons. Mackenzie (1978, ch. 4) has
discussed the formation and functions of hierarchies in structures.

The data reported by Pfeffer and Leblebici
(1973) provide some support for the position
that competition tends to produce more tightly
controlled organizational structures. Controlling for organizational size, the authors reported that competition was significantly and
positively associated with both frequency of
reporting by department heads and the amount
of formalization in the organization (1973, p.
275). Of even more interest, the data indicated
that competition interacts with dimensions of
technology and the organizational environment
to determine structure. Specifically, dimensions that were generally thought to lead to
decentralized, more differentiated, less formalized structures, such as the number of products or the number of product changes (Harvey,
1968; Thompson, 1967, ch. 6) only had the predicted effects in less competitive settings.
Heterogeneity and change did not affect structure as predicted in competitive environments.

The effect of competition to increase demand
for control, with the resultant increase in
centralization and formalization, is not as
surprising as it might first appear. We can all
think of organizations in which there is a
great deal of slack, typically operating under
conditions of little or limited competition.
When the situation changes, and the slack begins to diminish, control in the organization
is typically tightened. Practices and procedures are analyzed, discretion is reduced, and
control is increased. This response can be seen
in organizations ranging from universities to
business firms. Indeed, one of the reasons
people might want to work in organizations

facing limited competition and in which there is a lot of slack is because of the decreased pressure and greater discretion and latitude in behavior likely to be permitted in such settings.

UNCERTAINTY, THE ENVIRONMENT, AND STRUCTURE

Although very few researchers have investigated dependence and competition as determinants of organizational structure, uncertainty is a characteristic of the environment that has had a central role in discussions of organizational design. Burns and Stalker (1961) and Dill (1958) were among the first to examine and discuss different structural arrangements in organizations. In a case study of two Norwegian firms, Dill (1958) argued that the stability and certainty of the organization's environment affected managerial autonomy. Burns and Stalker systematically described two types of organizational structures—the mechanistic and the organic. The mechanistic structure was characterized by well-defined roles, a clear hierarchy of authority, the presence of formal rules and procedures, and a more orderly and controlled decision process. It would not be much of an exaggeration to note that most of the characteristics of the mechanistic form of organization also describe bureaucracy, as outlined by Weber (1947). The organic structure, on the other hand, was nonbureaucratic. There was a more fluid, less formalized structure, characterized by overlapping role assignments, fewer rules and formal procedures, and a more consultative form of decision-making. Recently, Hage and Aiken (1970) have empirically indicated that the characteristics outlined by Burns and Stalker do tend to occur together, almost defining organizational structural types. However, the one-dimensional or multidimensional nature of the structures and the types described remains open to debate (see, e.g., Hall, 1963, Pugh et al., 1969).

Part of the reason for the confusion as to whether there is just one dimension describing structure, mechanistic or organic, or otherwise called bureaucratic or nonbureaucratic, or whether structural features do not cluster together but constitute separate dimensions of design, lies in problems in methodology and the interpretation of results. Multivariate analysis, particularly factor analysis, has been used extensively in these studies. Given more observations than variables, one can always compute a factor structure from a set of variables. Furthermore, if one uses orthogonal rotation, which is what is customarily done, one ends up with orthogonal, uncorrelated factors. Thus, using factor analysis with orthogonal rotation to test whether bureaucracy is a unidimensional or multidimensional concept tends to presuppose the result, particularly when one uses variables with measurement error so that correlations will be less than perfect in any event.

Clearly, most of the management literature, and the literature on designing organizations, has operated from a unidimensional perspective. Moreover, the literature has been, invariably, biased in favor of the organic, nonbureaucratic organizational forms. Bennis (1964) has gone so far as to predict the end of bureaucracy, and most of the other advocates have been strong in their advocacy of organic, decentralized, less formalized structures (see, e.g., Likert, 1967; Miles, 1975).

These authors have all argued, from the original Burns and Stalker (1961) research, that structures are contingent, with environmental uncertainty being the principal determinant of structure. In uncertain, rapidly changing environments, the argument proceeds, decentralized, organic, nonbureaucratic structures are required (Duncan, 1972; Miles, 1975). Thus, since the world is becoming more turbulent and uncertain, there will be an increasing tendency for organizational designs to be nonbureaucratic. Further, the argument is made that the cost of using an organic structure, when a mechanistic one would be sufficient, is inefficiency and excess costs. But, the consequence of having a mechanistic structure under conditions of uncertainty may be organizational failure. Given the assymetrical consequences of the use of an appropriate structure, the argument is made that managers should design structures that err on the side of the organic or nonbureaucratic.

Other authors can also be mustered to support the preceding line of reasoning. Weick (1969), for example, argued that organizations are, above all, information-processing systems. In order to register equivocality (uncertainty), the organizational processes (assembly rules for interlocked cycles of behavior) must have equivocality (uncertainty). This is a direct variant of Ashby's (1956) law of requisite variety, and argues that to register and cope with uncertainty, uncertain processes, and presumably uncertain structures, are required. Thompson (1967) also has argued that rapidly changing environments, presumably uncertain environments, are associated with decentralized decision-making in the boundary-spanning units dealing with the environment. Indeed, the notion of structures contingent on environment, with uncertainty being the critical dimension, is becoming almost a noncontingent truism in management writing.

There are several problems with these analyses, however. First, as we have already mentioned, whether or not structures are unidimensional is an issue open to continuing debate. If structural patterns are not unidimensional, then the descriptions of contingency theory we find liberally represented in the literature are, at best, oversimplified. Statements like, "uncertain environments require organic structural arrangements," will have to be modified to include the several aspects of structure, rather than a single, ideal description. The second problem with these analyses, as Child (1972) has cogently noted, is that they assume

a determinism which is simply at variance with
observed reality. Not only do organizations
operating in ostensibly similar environments
have different structures but they may even be
equally successful. Third, following Ashby's
(1956) suggestion, if it takes uncertainty to
register uncertainty, one might make the argument that perceptions of environmental complexity and uncertainty are *consequences* of organizational designs, rather than causes. Weick
(1969) has argued that environments are enacted, created by a process of attention. It
is plausible to argue that differentiated
structures will perceive a heterogeneous environment, or that decentralized structures
will perceive more environmental uncertainty as
a consequence of the structural arrangements.

Finally, the basic model of organization,
underlying models such as those of Bennis,
Likert, and Miles, is one that presumes a goal
of efficiency or effectiveness, and a consensus
on both objectives and a definition of reality
which is possibly at variance with the real
world. The models suggested are good management ideology, but they are also highly ideal-
ized prescriptions and descriptions of actual
organizational life. Bennis himself seems to
be coming to this conclusion. After serving
as a vice-president of the State University of
New York at Buffalo, Bennis now has come to
question whether persons really desire participation, and more fundamentally, whether bureaucracy is really on its way out (Bennis, 1974).
Indeed, one might argue that the elements of
bureaucracy are becoming more pervasive in organizations. Certainly, there are increasing
rules and procedures concerned with hiring and
personnel, and more formalized mechanisms of
review of both individual and subunit performance. Ironically, pleas for justice and due
process in organizational decision-making have
led to quasijudicial systems, complete with
formal rules and procedures, and a limitation
rather than an expansion of discretion on the
part of all concerned.

Miles (1975) emphasized the importance of management orientation as a way out of the problem of environmental determinism. But management orientation can be translated, probably, as management attitudes, and the literature on the relationship between attitudes and behavior leads one to argue that this is not likely to be a productive line of inquiry either, at least in a causal sense. Attitudes are as likely to be a consequence of the existing structure as they are to be a cause of it.

Uncertainty presumably refers to events that the organization cannot forecast. But first, for uncertainty to concern the organization, the events must have consequences for the organization. Uncertainty, then, is problematic only when it occurs along with dependence. Second, uncertainty is unplanned variation. Mere change, or rate of change, is no guarantee that the situation is uncertain. Change, variation,. and a dynamic environment may all be capable of being predicted, in which case, there is no uncertainty. It is not the stability of the organization's environment that matters, then; it is the unpredicted change of variables that affect critical organizational dependencies.

Organizations have a variety of possible responses to uncertainty. Cyert and March (1963) argued that organizations seek to avoid uncertainty. By *avoidance* these authors meant avoidance in the truest sense—simply ignoring the uncertainty. The underlying concept was that those things that could not be predicted would not be taken into consideration in the formulation of organizational policies. It is fair to suggest that much individual behavior operates in a very similar fashion. Both in organizations and among people, there is very little long-range planning, at least that affects current actions.

Consistent with the avoidance-of-uncertainty argument, Cyert and March (1963) stated that organizations used simple standard operating procedures—simple rules and guidelines to make

decisions and to determine policy (see Tuggle,
1978). Much like other forms of avoidance,
simple rules and procedures ignore uncertainty.
One example of such a standard operating procedure is mark-up pricing. A retail store receives inventory from a supplier, which then
must be priced for sale. Theoretically, the
store could concern itself with allocating its
fixed costs to the items in inventory, and to
probable competitive pricing policies and
elasticity of consumers' demand. In practice,
most retail businesses operate on a fixed mark-
up percentage, which in retail furniture and
jewelry typically is 100%. This means that the
store owner simply takes the invoice price
from the supplier and doubles it to obtain the
price he will charge. Although the complexities
and uncertainties of the competitive market remain, the manager has chosen to ignore them and
operate using relatively simple and noncontingent decision rules.

An evolutionary model of organizational ecology would suggest that, in the long run, rules
that are not suited to environmental requirements will cause organizations to go out of
business, or else new rules will be learned.
In either the natural selection or operant
conditioning model of organizational functioning, adaptation occurs without conscious, or
at least necessarily accurate, planning or
decision-making by the organizational managers.
In the case of natural selection, those organizations employing nonadaptive decision-making
rules will fail, leaving only those that use
appropriate rules and structures. The learning
model suggests that organizations are selectively reinforced for using various rules or
structures, and learn them over time through a
process of conditioning. In both models, organizational adaptation is not necessarily an
intentional, planned process.

When environmental uncertainties are so critical that they cannot be ignored, organizations
may still attempt to isolate or manage their
effects. Thus, not all parts of an organization

need to be readily adaptable, only certain sec-
tions. The segmenting of organizations produces
organizations that are loosely coupled. Loosely coupled structures (Aldrich, 1974) may ab-
sorb environmental changes with a minimum of
change in other parts of the organization. A
university is a good example of a loosely
coupled organization. If there is a demand for
educational "relevance" or applied research,
or both, and the natural environment is a currently hot topic, the organization establishes
a school or research unit with that particular
focus. The rest of the university goes on unchanged, and the environmental demands are at
least partially met by a relatively minor, ad
hoc structural modification. If consumer activ-
ism is high, corporations may establish consumer affairs departments, again localizing the
effect of environmental contingencies. In
another context, Leeds (1964) has written of
protest absorption in organizations in an analogous fashion. Setting up special activities
or subunits, only loosely linked to other organizational activities, is a way of containing
both attempts at influence and the effects of
uncertainty on the organization.

Since uncertainty comes from unplanned variations, organizations can reduce uncertainty,
and their requirements for flexibility, by developing more accurate forecasting capabilities
and by increasing surveillance of the environment to be better informed. What is certain in
one organization may be uncertain in another,
given differences in information systems and
forecasting capabilities. The ability to predict future environmental contingencies means
that the organization can adapt on its own
terms, and does not need the same amount of
short term flexibility built into its structure and operations.

One of the most used and most successful organizational responses is to build in organizational slack (Cyert and March, 1963). If the
organization has enough excess or slack resources, or large enough size, it can afford to

be less immediately responsive to changes in
environmental demands. The storing of resources
against future contingencies means that organizations can use the slack to buffer the effects
of environmental fluctuations. Organizational
slack was recognized as a form of buffering by
Cyert and March, and slack resources may assure
organizational survival regardless of the organization's lack of flexibility.

It would be interesting to speculate on wny
bureaucracy, or mechanistic structures, have
survived and promise to increase, in spite of
the early predictions to the contrary. It
should be clear that there are many possible
organizational responses to uncertainty besides developing organic structures, even in a
turbulent and uncertain environment. Organizations may avoid uncertainty, and can do so as
long as they possess sufficient slack resources; further, as loosely coupled systems,
organizations can localize the effects of influence or uncertainty, responding with minor
structural adaptations, such as adding a new
unit. Furthermore, organizations can reduce uncertainty by forecasting and surveillance, as
well as by managing the environment.

As usually characterized, organic structures
represent examples of power equalization (see,
e.g., Leavitt, 1965). Power is not dispersed
voluntarily, we would suggest, nor is power
dispersed solely in response to uncertainty,
which after all is enacted and therefore can
be selectively controlled. Power is dispersed
when subordinates, the organizational parti-
sans, achieve favorable dependence relationships with respect to higher organizational
managers. This may occur as in the case of
Crozier's (1964) maintenance engineers, because the participants can close down the
plant, or because they control the most critical resources or performances needed in the
organization. Hierarchies remain stable because, in their pure form, they may be quite
efficient (see Mackenzie, 1978). Since hierarchies may be easier to control politically,

disputes are reduced, and when they occur, conflicts are less destructive. Organic structures have not come to dominate organizations simply because those in control have been able, thus far, to maintain their control.

REFERENCES

Aiken, Michael and Hage, Jerald. "Organizational Interdependence and Intra-Organizational Structure." *American Sociological Review 33* (1968): 912-30.

Aldrich, Howard. "The Environment as a Network of Organizations: Theoretical and Methodological Implications." Presented to the Research Committee on Organizations Section, International Sociological Association, Toronto, Canada, August, 1974.

Ashby, W. R. *An Introduction to Cybernetics*. New York: John Wiley, 1956.

Bennis, Warren G. "Organizational Development and the Fate of Bureaucracy." Invited Address, American Psychological Association, Los Angeles, California, September 4, 1964.

_____. "A Funny Thing Happened on the Way to the Future." In *Organizations of the Future*, edited by H. Leavitt, L. Pinfield, and E. Webb, pp. 3-28. New York: Praeger, 1974.

Blau, Peter M. *Exchange and Power in Social Life*. New York: John Wiley, 1964.

Burns, Tom, and Stalker, G. M. *The Management of Innovation*. London: Tavistock, 1961.

Child, John. "Organizational Structure, Environment and Performance: The Role of Strategic Choice." *Sociology 6* (1972): 2-22.

Crozier, Michel. *The Bureaucratic Phenomenon*. Chicago: University of Chicago Press, 1964.

Cyert, Richard M., and March, James G. *A Behavioral Theory of the Firm*. Englewood Cliffs, N.J.: Prentice-Hall, 1963.

Dill, W. R. "Environment as an Influence on Managerial

Autonomy." *Administrative Science Quarterly 2* (1958): 409-43.

Dowling, John, and Pfeffer, Jeffrey. "Organizational Legitimacy: Social Values and Organizational Behavior." *Pacific Sociological Review 18* (1975): 122-36.

Duncan, Robert B. "Characteristics of Organizational Environments and Perceived Environmental Uncertainty." *Administrative Science Quarterly 17* (1972): 313-27.

Emerson, Richard M. "Power-Dependence Relations." *American Sociological Review 27* (1962): 31-41.

Hage, Jerald, and Aiken, Michael. *Social Change in Complex Organizations*. New York: Random House, 1970.

Hall, Richard H. "The Concept of Bureaucracy: An Empirical Assessment." *American Journal of Sociology 69* (1963): 32-40.

Harvey, Edward. "Technology and the Structure of Organizations." *American Sociological Review 33* (1968): 247-59.

Hunt, Raymond, G., and Hunt, Gregory W. "Some Structural Features of Relations Between the Department of Defense, the National Aeronautics and Space Administration, and their Principal Contractors." *Social Forces 49* (1971): 414-31.

Inkson, J. H. K.; Pugh, D. S.; and Hickson, D. J.: "Organization Context and Structure: An Abbreviated Replication." *Administrative Science Quarterly 15* (1970): 318-29.

Jacobs, David. "Dependency and Vulnerability: An Exchange Approach to the Control of Organizations." *Administrative Science Quarterly 19* (1974): 45-59.

Katz, Daniel, and Kahn, Robert L. *The Social Psychology of Organizations*. New York: John Wiley, 1966.

Korten, David C. "Situational Determinants of Leadership Structure." *Journal of Conflict Resolution 6* (1962): 222-35.

Lawrence, Paul R., and Lorsch, Jay W. *Developing Organizations: Diagnosis and Action*. Reading, Mass.: Addison-Wesley, 1969.

Leavitt, Harold J. "Applied Organizational Change In Industry: Structural, Technological and Humanistic Approaches." In *Handbook of Organizations*, edited by James G. March, 1144-70. Chicago: Rand McNally, 1965.

Leeds, Ruth. "The Absorption of Protest: A Working Paper." In *New Perspectives in Organization Research*, edited by W. W. Cooper, H. G. Leavitt, and M. W. Shelly, pp. 115-35. New York: Wiley, 1964.

Likert, Rensis. *The Human Organization*. New York: McGraw-Hill, 1967.

Mackenzie, Kenneth D. *Organizational Structures*. Arlington Heights, Ill.: AHM Publishing Corporation, 1978.

Miles, Raymond E. *Theories of Management: Implications for Organizational Behavior and Development*. New York: McGraw-Hill, 1975.

Mindlin, Sergio E., and Aldrich, Howard. "Interorganizational Dependence: A Review of the Concept and a Re-Examination of the Findings of the Aston Group." *Administrative Science Quarterly 20* (1975): 382-92.

Pfeffer, Jeffrey. *Organizational Ecology: A System Resource Approach*. Ann Arbor: University of Michigan Microfilms, 1972.

Pfeffer, Jeffrey, and Leblebici, Huseyin. "The Effect of Competition on Some Dimensions of Organizational Structure." *Social Forces 52* (1973): 268-79.

Pfeffer, Jeffrey, and Salancik, Gerald R. "Organizational Decision Making as a Political Process: The Case of a University Budget." *Administrative Science Quarterly 19* (1974): 135-51.

Pugh, D. S.; Hickson, D. J.; Hinings, C.; and Turner, C. "The Context of Organization Structures." *Administrative Science Quarterly 14* (1969): 91-124.

Salancik, Gerald R., and Pfeffer, Jeffrey. "The Bases and Use of Power in Organizational Decision Making: The Case of a University." *Administrative Science Quarterly 19* (1974): 453-73.

Stern, Robert N., and Reynolds, W. Jeff. "Organizational Change and the Social Control of Institutions: The Regulation of Intercollegiate Athletics." Unpublished

Ms. Ithaca: New York State School of Industrial and Labor Relations, 1974.

Thibaut, John, and Kelley, Harold H. *The Social Psychology of Groups*. New York: John Wiley, 1959.

Thompson, James D. "Organizations and Output Transactions." *American Journal of Sociology 68* (1962): 309-24.

_____. *Organizations in Action*. New York: McGraw-Hill, 1967.

Tuggle, Francis D. *Organizational Processes*. Arlington Heights, Ill.: AHM Publishing Corporation, 1978.

Weber, M. *The Theory of Social and Economic Organization*. New York: Oxford University Press, 1947.

Weick, Karl E. *The Social Psychology of Organizing*. Reading, Mass.: Addison-Wesley, 1969.

Wiley, Mary Glenn, and Zald, Mayer N. "The Growth and Transformation of Educational Accrediting Agencies: An Exploratory Study in Social Control of Institutions." *Sociology of Education 41* (1968): 36-56.

6

Designing the Environment to Fit the Organization

Organizational structures represent the distribution of control, the division of labor and responsibility, in an organization. Organizational redesign, the making of major structural modifications, is a major organizational dislocation. Anyone who has ever witnessed a major organization change knows what we mean. People fight to maintain their power, their responsibilities, and their positions. Once the balance of control is disturbed, all participants engage in a struggle to enhance their relative positions. Structural change comes about only rarely, primarily because of the amount of conflict and uncertainty it brings with it.

Organizations, therefore, seek to manage environmental uncertainty, dependence, and competition to avoid having to make structural and technological responses. Rather than designing the organization to "fit" the environment (the position of the contingency theorists), it is more likely that first the organization will attempt to design its environment to fit its present structural arrangements. Structural change involves the renegotiation of internal relationships, which is to be avoided.

MANAGING COMPETITION

One source of uncertainty, and an important form of interdependence, arises from competitive relationships. All organizations compete for resources, and organizations, both business and nonbusiness, compete to attract qualified personnel as well as support. Elesh (1973), for instance, has described the dimensions of the competition among universities for students. Indeed, because of the generalized competition for resources, Yuchtman and Seashore (1967) have suggested that organizational effectiveness can be assessed by how well the organization fares in obtaining resources.

Competition poses an external threat to the organization. The possibility of organizational failure as a consequence of being unable to maintain one's position in situations of competition is a serious threat. Organizations can make two possible responses. First, they can become efficient or effective enough to ensure success in the competitive battle. Second, they can enter into relationships with competitors to limit the severity, scope, and danger posed by the competition. The latter course is more likely. As we have already noted, organizations prefer not to undertake major structural adjustments. More important, the first strategy leads to a cycle of competitive response among organizations. One cannot be sure, regardless of the level of efficiency achieved, that another organization will not come up with some innovation that will again place the focal organization at a competitive disadvantage. Much like a price war, unrestrained competition is endless, boundless, and threatening to organizational survival. Given organizational desires for certainty and predictability, for which organizations are apparently willing to trade profit (see, e.g., Caves, 1970), it is only natural that organizations will evolve ways of managing competitive relationships.

The development of norms tending to restrain competition, or limit its scope, is something that may occur spontaneously in a group of interacting competitor organizations. Weick (1969), following Allport (1962), has written of the development of interlocked cycles of behavior, or group structures to which group members conform. Weick has argued that one of the reasons for the development of such structures is that each group member believes that by conforming and belonging to the group, he will fare better than outside of the group. Group membership, with the predictability in relationships that follows, reduces uncertainty for the members. Further, as long as outcomes are above what they might receive in alternative collective structures, there is no reason not to remain and conform.

Competitors are interdependent, assuming there are relatively few of them. In such a situation of interdependence, behavior is likely to become coordinated even without overt actions taken to link the organizations together. Rabinowitz et al. (1966) experimentally indicated how, in a situation in which payoffs were interdependent, two people developed a stable pattern of interaction without any communication. Phillips (1960) has noted that as the number of social units to be coordinated increases, more formal mechanisms of coordination must be employed, since informal arrangements will no longer be as effective. And, with very large numbers of organizations, interdependence between any two becomes relatively small, so that in market situations approaching perfect competition, the organization no longer finds it feasible to coordinate behavior with the large number of possible competitors and again behaves as if there were no interdependence in the situation.

With a small number of relevant competitors, norms and patterns of behavior tending to limit competition can develop without overt communication, or even without informal interorganizational linkage mechanisms. Such norm development and the attaining of stable, consistent patterns of interaction are enhanced to the extent that the organizations involved are staffed with managers with similar backgrounds, information, and values. One of the functions of professional education, in any profession, is the inculcation of professionally relevant norms and standards of behavior. Just as some professional groups learn group solidarity, making it hard to find members to testify against fellow professionals at trials (see, e.g., Kessel, 1958), so a common background and professional training may enhance the development of collective structures among the managers of business firms (see, Kiesler, 1978).

That competition is bounded is illustrated by the example provided by Perrow (1970, pp. 24-25). He noted that when a company's manufacturing facility burned down, competitors, rather than attempting to take the business away while the facility was being repaired, offered the firm the use of their manufacturing facilities in the off-shifts, permitting the company to remain in business as a competitor while the plant was being rebuilt. Furthermore, examples of price leadership abound, in which firms follow each other's pricing, and compete only in such matters as advertising or product attributes. The development of an identity with the profession of management, accomplished through training in business school, must serve, like other professional education, to build some community of interest and feeling among the management group. This community of interest is enhanced through trade and business associations, as well as through common service on various charitable and civic organizations' boards of directors.

In addition to the development of norms regulating behavior, somewhat more formal interorganizational linkage may be undertaken to structure interorganizational behavior. Organizations may be linked together through interlocking directorates, the movement of executive personnel among organizations, joint ventures, trade or industry associations, and by actual price-fixing and market-sharing conspiracies. Finally competitive interdependence can be totally absorbed through merger.

We have argued that the development of collective structures of behavior among organizations without communication can occur only when there are relatively few participants, so that stable and accurate conjectural variations, or estimates of the likely response of each organization to the other, can arise. Tacit, informal coordination is harder to maintain in larger groups. Similarly, as the number of social units increases, the need for more formalized, planned structures to maintain coordination increases. Thus, in the study of organizational structures, a positive relationship has been observed, for instance, between size and the degree of formalization (Meyer, 1972). Furthermore, with very large numbers of actors, the likelihood that several linkages among them will provide much organization or structure is reduced. Consequently, we have argued that interorganizational linkages, accomplished on the basis of pairs, will be most evident in situations in which there is some intermediate range of concentration, or when the number of major competitors is intermediate.

In studies of joint ventures (Pfeffer and Nowak, 1976), mergers (Pfeffer, 1972b), the movement of executive personnel among organizations (Pfeffer and Leblebici, 1973), and the interlocking of directorates (Pfeffer and Nowak, 1975), the proposition developed above

has been consistently supported. In each instance, there is a higher incidence of interaction, using the form of interorganizational
linkage being examined, among competitor organizations in environments of intermediate
concentration, or when there are an intermediate number of major competing organizations.

Thus, for example, the movement of executive
personnel among organizations in the same industry (Pfeffer and Leblebici, 1973) is more
frequent when there are an intermediate number
of organizations. The linking of competitors
through paired mechanisms of interaction is
consistently related to the environmental dimensions measuring the necessity and possibility of developing collective structures through
such interaction. This perspective explains
more than other arguments related to the size
of the organization, industry technology, or
industry growth, and operates consistently
across various kinds of interorganizational behavior.

In each instance of interorganizational linkage, organizations become bound together
through an interpenetration of personnel, as in
the case of executive movement or interlocking
directorates, or through a pooling of assets,
as in the case of joint ventures. Of course,
in merger, the organizations become completely
unified under common ownership and control.
Merger, then, is one end of the scale of absorption, with the interlocking of directors
probably the other end, involving a limited absorption of one representative by the other
organization. In each instance as well, a
mechanism is established whereby information
can be exchanged. The exchange of information
is most essential in developing effective coordinated behavior.

The information-exchange role is why trade
associations are another way for developing a
collective structure among a group of organizations. Trade associations typically provide a
pooling and sharing of cost and market information, and act as representative for the

organizations in issues of common interest. The association, then, promotes a common identification, through the vehicle of membership with competitors in the association. This common identification is further enhanced through the development and presentation of industry viewpoints on issues of concern, and through the definition of issues in collective terms. Further, through information sharing, particularly in the areas of research and development, costs, and market information, common information and values can be developed, to enhance further the likelihood of the development of a collective structure of interorganizational behavior. Although trade associations have not received the empirical attention given to other forms of interorganizational linkage, they are important mechanisms of interorganizational coordination.

The issue of the purposefulness of these interorganizational strategies of linkage must be addressed. If one talks to business managers of organizations engaging in recruitment, nominating directors, or undertaking joint ventures, one does not hear the language of interfirm coordination or the development of collective structures. To what extent, then, can these activities be viewed as organizational strategies, undertaken to manage competitive interdependence?

First, many of the reasons given for business behavior can be translated into the idea of developing interfirm organizations. Recruitment, for example, may be undertaken with the goal of hiring the best candidate. However, *best* may mean different things, depending on the context of the organization. *Best* in an organization in an oligopolistic situation, we suggest, is likely to mean someone with experience in the industry, familiar with the competitive circumstances that make the job of organizational management particularly problematic. In an industry with only one firm, recruitment from within the industry is not possible, unless it is recruitment from within the same organization. In settings with many competitors, one does not hear much about knowledge of the competitive environment; rather, the emphasis may be on internal administrative capabilities or technical skills. Second the ecological perspective (Hannan and Freeman, 1976), borrowing from the biological analogy, would argue that intention is not the critical variable. If the use of strategies to reduce competition is appropriate, such strategies will be selected by environmental variations. Third, although most of the studies have used a modeling approach, in which a motivation or rationale is assumed, empirical predictions consistent with this perspective are derived, and are then compared with empirical data, some direct evidence on the effects of some of these interorganizational linkages is available. Mead (1967) for example, examined joint bidding for oil and gas leases. He reported that there was a significant reduction in competitive bidding for the same tract in sales in which the particular organizations had jointly bid on other tracts. Further, the reduction in competitive bidding against firms that were partners in other bidding arrangements persisted for up to two years after the partnership. Since there was evidence that the price of the lease was inversely related to the number of bidders, the reduction in competitive behavior was both observable and consequential in this instance.

Unfortunately, the effects of these strategies for managing competitive interdependence have not been examined. Hirsch (1975) has argued for the importance of the organization's institutional environment as a determinant of organizational success. It would seem that one form of uncertainty avoidance, discussed by Cyert and March (1963), is to manage the environment to assure favorable and stable competitive relationships.

REGULATION TO REDUCE COMPETITION

Another method for coping with competitive interdependence involves using the power of the government to stabilize relationships among competitors. There are two general conceptions of administrative regulation. One theory is that regulation is adopted to protect the interests of the general public. Although occasionally decisions are made in error or administrative agencies do not adequately fulfill this function of public service, according to this argument serving the general public interest is the underlying goal of administrative regulation, and appropriate reforms or structural readjustments should be undertaken to remedy the problems. The second theory argues that administrative regulation is acquired by the regulated occupation or industry and operated for its benefit and with its support. This view holds that reform of the regulatory process to serve the public interest is virtually impossible, given the underlying purpose of the organization and its contingencies, which require accommodation with the regulated industry. Bernstein (1955) has argued that regulatory agencies have a definable life cycle in which the agency, when first established, operates with vigor in the public interest, over time becomes an institutionalized and integral part of the industrial order, and loses its original fervor and identification with regulation for the public benefit.

The evidence on the effects of regulation (see, e.g., Jordan, 1972; Pfeffer, 1974b) is consistent with the view that regulation operates typically to benefit those being regulated. In terms of managing competitive interdependence, there is evidence that regulation can, and does, operate to deal with several competitive problems, including the entry of competitors and the possibility of price competition.

Many regulatory authorities have the power to restrict entry into the industry or occupation. This power to restrict entry has been used, it appears, to reduce the number of competitors below what it might have been in the absence of such restriction. Since the

reduction in the number of competitors will,
with other things being equal, lead to both
higher profits and a more stable industry
structure, entry restriction helps organizations cope with competitive interdependence.
Peltzman (1965) has found that as a result of
restriction of entry into commercial banking,
there has probably been more than a 50% decrease in the number of commercial banks
founded compared to what might have been expected based on the profitability characteristics of the industry. Jordan (1970) noted that
after the founding of the Civil Aeronautics
Board in 1938, no new national carriers were
permitted, and the only entrants to the airline
industry were those created in a local service
experiment in the 1940s. Stigler (1971) and
Volotta (1967) both examined the effect of the
Interstate Commerce Commission on restriction
of entry into the trucking industry. Both
found substantial effects on the reduction of
the number of competitors compared to what
might be expected in the absence of regulation.
   The effect of occupational licensing to restrict entry into occupations was first examined by Friedman and Kuznets (1945). Holen
(1965) has shown that licensing arrangements
that restrict interstate mobility of professionals lead to larger than expected income
differentials among professionals practicing
in different states. Both Holen (1965) and
Pfeffer (1974a) provided evidence that occupational incomes were positively related to the
difficulty of entry into the occupation in
a state, measured by the proportion of persons
applying who failed to obtain licenses. Entry
restriction also has operated in the electric
utility and telephone industries, as well as
in television and telecommunication.
   While the restriction of entry certainly enhances the ability of organizations to manage
competitive interdependence by reducing the
number of competitors, it is still true that
competition may occur, leading to the possibility of the failure of one or more of the

organizations. Regulation, as it has been
employed, effectively eliminates price competition, and frequently also serves to restrict
other forms of competition as well. Jordan
(1970) compared airline fares within
California, which are not regulated by the CAB,
with fares charged by airlines which operated
on an interstate basis, and hence were regulated, as well as with comparable routes and
distances elsewhere. He estimated that, in the
absence of regulation, air fares in the
California market were 24% or more lower than
what they would be with complete CAB regulation. Keeler (1972) estimated cost functions
for the airlines for a variety of major routes
in the United States. Allowing for a reasonable
rate of return in excess of the costs, Keeler
found that there were substantially higher
prices with regulation, with the amount of the
overcharge occasionally as much as 80%. Sloss
(1970) compared trucking rates in Canada between provinces in which there was regulation
and those in which trucking was not regulated.
He estimated that rates in provinces without
regulation were about 9% - 12% lower. Farmer
(1964) compared differences in rates charged
for regulated and unregulated shipping of
agricultural products, and found revenues and
costs per inter-city ton-mile far lower for
those agricultural carriers exempt from regulation.

Regulatory agencies provide the coercion of
the government to police the restriction of
competition which they create. The maintenance
of collective structures of behavior to reduce
competitive interdependence is always problematic. In any group or cartel, there will be
deviants, particularly when there may be
strong economic incentives, at least in the
short term, for such deviation. Williamson
(1965) has noted the dynamic nature of cartel
behavior, with the interfirm group continually
forming and reforming. With the power of the
state, however, group maintenance becomes much
less problematic. This was illustrated in a

study by MacAvoy (1965) of railroad rates in
the late 1800s. MacAvoy observed, using
archival data, a pattern of rate fluctuation
on the route from Chicago to the East coast,
as the railroad cartel formed and set prices,
and then fell apart as members attempted to
charge lower prices to obtain more business.
The fluctuation in freight rates was extreme,
varying as much as 100% between the low and
the high rates charged, depending on whether
the cartel was operating or not. After the
creation of the ICC in 1887, MacAvoy documents
a new stability in the freight rates, govern-
mentally imposed, at an amount somewhat higher
than the previously highest cartel rate.

The use of governmental authority to maintain
structured interorganizational behavior is an
alternative to the use of the various informal
linkage mechanisms previously discussed. When
employed, it has the danger of permanently
permitting political intervention in organizational operations. However, apparently many
organizations have found this risk worth
bearing.

MANAGING SYMBIOTIC INTERDEPENDENCE

In addition to facing competitive interdependence, in which organizational survival
is affected by the actions of competing organizations, organizations also have vertical
interdependence with supplier and customer
groups and organizations. This interdependence,
resulting from dependence on organizations
engaging in different but complementary activities that the focal organization requires, is
called symbiotic interdependence (Hawley,
1950). The acquisition of necessary inputs and
the disposal of output is required for the
continuing cycle of organizational activity,
and therefore, symbiotic interdependence also
requires organizational action.

Many of the same activities that organizations may employ to manage competitive

interdependence can also be used to restructure the environment to cope with symbiotic interdependence. Pfeffer (1972b) has examined merger behavior among large industrial firms. He reported that patterns of merger activity among industry sectors were not correlated with profit rates or levels of industrial concentration, but rather were significantly related to patterns of resource exchange. Based on these results, he concluded that merger behavior could be explained as a response to symbiotic as well as competitive interdependence. As in the case of competitive interdependence, merger among vertically related organizations enables the new, enlarged organization to have more of its critical contingencies within its boundaries, and hence, more subject to its control.

Joint ventures, involving only a partial pooling of assets, are less complete forms of absorbing uncertainty. Pfeffer and Nowak (1976), examining joint ventures among industrial sectors, found that, as in the case of mergers, patterns of joint venture activity corresponded to patterns of resource exchange, and were also predictable by the level of technology in the industry, measured by the proportion of research and development personnel to total employment. Joint ventures were more likely, then, to the extent that industries exchanged resources and to the extent that the industry had a high level of technology. In comparison with mergers, Pfeffer and Nowak reported that joint ventures, less frequently prosecuted under the antitrust laws, were more frequently used in coping with competitive interdependence, and less frequently used in coping with symbiotic interdependence.

Businesses and other organizations use the board of directors to coopt representatives of organizations with which they have transactions. Zald (1967) has noted that YWCA's in Chicago had board compositions reflecting the demographic composition of the areas served. Zald noted that because the supply of

relatively wealthy directors was restricted
in some areas, the organizations operating in
those areas were at a disadvantage. Price
(1963) examined the buffering function of the
boards of the Oregon Fish and Game Commis-
sions, arguing that the principal function
served was to negotiate the relationship between these organizations and their environments.

In a series of studies covering both business
and other organizations, Pfeffer has indicated
that the size, composition, and function of the
organization's board of directors can be explained by considerations of linkage with the
social environment. In a study of the boards
of directors of business firms, Pfeffer (1972a)
found that the size of the board was positively
related to the size of the organization and to
whether or not it was in a regulated industry;
the proportion of outside directors was also
related to the size of the firm and to whether
or not it was regulated. The proportion of
directors from financial institutions was
found to be positively related to the proportion of debt in the firm's capital structure.
Examining hospital boards of directors, Pfeffer
(1973) found that the size and function of the
board was related to the hospital's ownership
and source of funds. Privately owned hospitals
relying on donations for capital and operating
funds emphasized the linkage functions of the
board, and tended to have boards of directors
composed of people who could help raise money.
Allen (1974) has also noted the function of
boards of directors in linking organizations
together.

Yet another way of stabilizing interdependence is through the use of long-term contracts. To the extent that such contracts are
binding and enforceable, organizations remove
some of their problematic dependence on other
organizations. Forward contracting presumably
serves the interests of both parties, assuring
the purchasing organization an assured source
of supply and price, and assuring the selling

organization a customer and price. Such forward
contracting has been frequently used, particularly in the instances of critical and scarce
raw materials, such as coal and natural gas,
or in the case of products that have very long
lead times to build, such as electric genera-
tors.

Interdependence can presumably be avoided
also through a process of diversification. By
diversifying the organization's product line,
the firm can reduce its dependence on any single customer, or on suppliers that provide input necessary for the previously manufactured
product. Diversification is an observed and
likely response when organizations face situations of dependence that cannot be adequately
managed through merger, joint ventures, or cooptation. The aerospace manufacturers are examples of organizations that faced a highly
concentrated market with very few purchasers.
As a consequence, many of them tried, albeit
often unsuccessfully, to diversify into other
markets to reduce their dependence on their
few present customers.

Diversification is also observed in nonbusiness organizations. Colleges and universities have expanded their domains when necessary, to include both sexes as students, and
to add additional professional education and
other programs when that was necessary to avoid
dependence on either single or declining markets. Social service organizations also frequently attempt to add functions (Downs, 1967),
to ensure that regardless of changing perceptions of the need for social services, the organization's growth and survival can be maintained. The expansion of domain, as part of
a strategy of diversification to lessen the
organization's dependence on one sphere of
activity, is a general phenomenon observed for
both business and nonbusiness organizations.

Normative standards of behavior also control
the interaction among symbiotically interdependent organizations. Noncontractual relations
among organizations (Macaulay, 1963), based on

standard codes of conduct, serve to limit the use of dependence to control another organization's behavior, and tend to make relations among organizations more predictable. One such norm is reciprocity, which means that an act organization *A* performs for some other organization, *B*, creates for *B* the obligation to reciprocate in some fashion. It is a tenet of exchange theory that unbalanced exchanges are inherently unstable. Although this may not be true as the exchanges may be mandated, the concept of reciprocity does have strong normative foundations and acts as an important determinant of behavior. Perrow (1970) has related how organizations have attempted to systematize and enforce the norm of reciprocity through the use of trade relations personnel. Typically, large organizations make a variety of products and require a number of inputs. It is not at all uncommon, then, to have a situation in which an organization makes something required by another organization and at the same time requires some product that the other organization sells. If the first organization buys from the other it is the job of the trade relations people to ensure that this other buys what it can from the first. While such reciprocal arrangements are not legal under antitrust laws, since they constitute tying arrangements, they are nevertheless enforced by both organizations and the general norm of reciprocity. Such reciprocal exchanges tend to create mutual dependence among organizations, stabilizing interorganizational relationships while leaving the relationship relatively balanced.

Managing Uncertainty

We have discussed organizational actions that can be taken to manage competitive and symbiotic interdependence with other organizations. Such interdependence is one cause of uncertainty confronted by the organization.

Indeed, uncertainty without interdependence is not a problem for the organization, because it is only the organization's need for a particular exchange that causes problems when that exchange is uncertain. Uncertainty can be dealt with in ways other than those previously discussed, and in ways that do not necessarily require structural modifications to enhance organizational flexibility.

Thompson (1967) has argued that the organization can insulate itself from the environment through the techniques of buffering, smoothing, and forecasting. In buffering, inventories of output or input are built up. Environmental uncertainties do not then impinge on the organization, which is continually working from and putting into inventory both input and output. Inventories within an organization lessen the interdependence among subunits, thereby requiring less coordination, and diminishing the likelihood of conflict (see, e.g., Galbraith, 1973). Similarly, inventories between the organization and its environment serve to uncouple the organization, lessening its short run interdependence and the requirements for short run adaptability. Buffering through the use of stockpiles of capital, input, or labor has the cost of carrying the investment in the excess resources. However, this cost must be balanced against the cost of structural modifications that would be required if the interdependence between the organization and its environment were not buffered.

In smoothing environmental fluctuations, the organization attempts to manage the environment to reduce variations to which the organization must then adapt. A good example of this smoothing is the use of off-season sales to promote demand for some product or service at a time when demand would otherwise be unusually low, such as sales of air conditioners in the winter, or skis in the summer. Smoothing is an example of creating and managing demand, and has been discussed by Galbraith (1967) as necessary when there are large organizations with relatively high fixed costs because of investment in heavy capital equipment. Smoothing of demand through price schedules to encourage off-peak usage occurs in the telephone industry, as well as in airlines and, to a lesser extent, in electric utilities.

As we noted previously, uncertainty connotes unplanned fluctuations. With the development of better forecasting technologies, what before was random variation can now be more accurately forecast. There is no reason to assume that forecasting capabilities are equal across organizations. It is, therefore, possible for two organizations to exist in the same "objective" environment, with one experiencing much less uncertainty than the other because of a relative advantage in forecasting ability. Again, the organization has a choice of strategic options available. Instead of undertaking structural modifications to enhance responsiveness, the organization can develop forecasting capability to facilitate planned rather than ad hoc responses.

As we noted when we discussed the management of competitive interdependence, there are analogies between the behavior occuring among organizations and interpersonal behavior, particularly with respect to developing collective structures of behavior. Phillips (1960) has written of interfirm behavior, comparing it to the process of group formation. One of the things that occurs in a group is the development of norms, and conformity to expected patterns of behavior within the group. Behavior, in other words, becomes organized and predictable. Such stable patterns of behavior are also likely to develop among organizations, motivated, as in the case of individuals, partly by the goal of reducing uncertainty for all of the actors. Organizations are willing to conform to emerging norms governing behavior, and to limit voluntarily the discretion in their behavior to reduce uncertainty for other organizations, with the expectation that other organizations will similarly act to reduce the uncertainty the focal organization faces. Unplanned variation in behaviors, then, may be reduced not only through forecasting or the use of interorganizational linkages, but also may be handled through the mutual, voluntary reduction in discretion, as organizations conform to norms and develop predictable, stable patterns of behavior, serving to reduce the uncertainty for all concerned.

ORGANIZATIONAL LEGITIMATION

Legitimacy, defined as a perceived congruence between social values and organizational products and actions, is a resource helpful to organizations. Illegitimate organizations do not have adequate claims on the right to use valued social resources. Legitimacy, on the other hand, ensures continued social approval and the ability of the organization to claim the resources required to continue its activities. Because legitimacy is important for organizational survival, organizations take steps to ensure their legitimacy, and at the same time use legitimacy as a competitive weapon.

Legitimacy is inevitably problematical. Social values and norms themselves change, but more importantly, the congruence between an organization's product or service and prevailing social norms is always open to question and interpretation. Thus, there may be a contest over the meaning of some observable action. Inside the organization we noted that control over information was important because of the importance of the capacity to define the meaning of organizational activity to enhance the power of subunits. Between organizations as well, the capacity to control the definition of organizational activity is critical, because it is through such interpretation of actions and products that organizational legitimacy or illegitimacy becomes established. This argument provides one explanation for the powerful position of the media. In a societal

sense, the media serve in much the same role as
does the information system within an organization, determining what will be noticed and how
the various actions will be perceived and interpreted. The importance of the media for
establishing organizational legitimacy is well
recognized. In a study of the composition of
the boards of directors of electric utilities,
Pfeffer (1974c) reported that the amount of
representation by persons from organizations
engaged in information dissemination was much
greater than the representation of such people
on the boards of randomly selected firms. The
electric utilities, as publicly regulated
firms, face particularly critical issues of
legitimation, and as a consequence, tend to
coopt more representatives of the media.

Legitimacy is also used in contests among
competitive organizational types. Legitimacy
cannot be raised as a claim against a competitive organization of the same type, but if
distinctions can be drawn that fundamentally
differentiate among organizations, legitimacy
can be claimed by one organization as a tactic
against competing organizations. For instance,
the legitimacy of profit-making business firms
participating in education and medical care has
been challenged by nonprofit organizations in
order to restrict competition. There is some
inherent conflict between education and profit-
making, in this view. The illegitimacy of
business firms in educational activities has
limited the influence of textbook manufacturers, and has particularly caused problems for
firms like Behavioral Research Laboratories
(formerly on the American Stock Exchange) that
have attempted to engage in contract education.
In such a system, particular learning objectives, such as a given level of reading or
mathematical skill, are given to the firm under
contract. The firm is paid according to the
original contract schedule and how well it suc-
ceeds in meeting the specified learning objectives. As reported several years ago in the
Saturday Review, the mixing of profit-making firms

with education was opposed by the established
educational groups, such as the teachers and
school administrators, whose power and jobs
were threatened by this innovation in educational technology. The claim of the illegitimacy of profit in education was asserted in
this contest over control of educational systems.

A similar situation may occur in the instance
of proprietary hospitals, operated for profit
by corporations. Again, a claim of illegitimacy may be asserted by the nonprofit organizations who are threatened by the new competition on the grounds that profit and health
care are incompatible. Most of the large
corporations operating hospitals have taken
particular care to forestall such claims of
illegitimacy, emphasizing the goals of quality
of care at a reasonable price in their pub-
lished materials. Claims of legitimacy may be
used, then, to protect the organization's domain against competitors. Used in such fashion,
social values are selectively interpreted to
be consistent or inconsistent with a given type
of organization's activity.

Organizations facing problems of perceived
legitimacy may take actions to ensure that they
will be perceived as legitimate. As described
by Dowling and Pfeffer (1975), the American
Institute for Foreign Study, in the business
of sending students abroad during the summer
for study, engaged in cooptation. This involved
setting up an advisory board including major
educational figures such as principals and
superintendents from important market areas.
Similarly, the Hospital Corporation of America
has an advisory panel of doctors, as well as
a few doctors on its board of directors. Legitimating activity, then, involves placing members of the profession or practitioners of the
activity on boards or committees of the organization. Legitimacy is conferred through association with these people.

Second, legitimation is accomplished through
the statement of legitimate goals. In the case

of AIFS, the goal was not stated to be making
profit for the associated travel organization,
New England Travel, but rather the cultural
development and education of the students.
Similarly, in the Hospital Corporation of
America report, the quality and delivery of
fairly priced medical services is emphasized
as an objective. By asserting socially valued
objectives, the organization may act to enhance
its own legitimacy.

Third, it is important for the organization
to legitimate the product. In the case of the
American Institute for Foreign Study, this involved listing the colleges and universities
at which participants in their high school
summer study programs had received academic
credit. Although AIFS was careful to note in
the third paragraph that such advanced standing
may have been received because of reasons other
than the study abroad, the presentation of an
impressive list of universities provided some
legitimation for the study activity, as well
as implicitly identifying these institutions
with AIFS. Methods that tend to identify an
organization with other institutions of established, unquestioned legitimacy also tend to
enhance the legitimacy of the organization in
question.

Finally, legitimacy is dependent on the use
of methods of operation that are perceived as
legitimate. In the case of AIFS, operating summer educational programs, legitimation involved
the use of the campuses of European universities and the development of rules and regulations consistent with those that might be expected in a school. The legitimacy of the production of a product or service is as important
as the legitimacy of the output itself. Social
values govern the use of appropriate technologies and means of organization, and people tend
to associate certain rules and procedures with
the production of particular outputs. Legitimacy is created by a perceived congruence between social values and organizational actions;

thus, the trappings must correspond to what is expected.

As with other organizational contingencies, legitimacy provides internal power to those within the organization who are capable of creating it. Since legitimacy is derived from the perception of organizational actions as congruent with predominant norms and values, those in the organization skilled in creating appropriate interpretations for actions are critical. Other things being equal, organizations in which legitimacy is problematic will probably tend to have relatively more powerful persons in boundary roles. Persons with skills in communication, or with access to contacts in the media, will also gain relatively more influence when legitimacy is a problem.

THE ORGANIZATION AS A POLITICAL ACTOR

In attempting to manage its environment, the organization may seek to use the coercive power of the state for its benefit. The involvement of corporations in politics has been competently described by Epstein (1969), and here we will only briefly delineate some of the ways in which the state acts to benefit organizations. Of course, to receive such benefits, organizations must make an investment—an investment of time and resources to influence the political process for its benefit. Frequently, benefits are distributed to all participants in an industry, in which case, industry associations may undertake some of the tasks of representing the organizations. In this instance, however, there is the problem of the free rider. If only some organizations join and contribute to an industry association which subsequently achieves some governmental action of benefit to the entire industry, all organizations receive the outcomes though only some incurred the costs. As long as an organization believes it is not going to harm the

organization's efforts by remaining outside of
the group, it is rational, using only economic
factors, for it to do so. This problem of the
free rider has been analyzed by Olson (1965)
and Stigler (1974).

As Stigler (1971) has noted, the government
can provide several kinds of benefits to an
organization. First, it can provide direct cash
subsidies. There are subsidies for builders of
ships, and air mail subsidies have been paid to
smaller airlines to keep them in business, even
though the amount of the subsidy was based on
financial need rather than on the amount of
mail carried. Without entry restriction, however, the subsidies will be divided among an
ever greater number of participants. Typically,
therefore, subsidies are paid only in industries where entry is restricted, either by
capital investment requirements as in ship-
building, or by regulation of entry, as in the
case of airlines.

Political action also affects the conditions
of trade, including the amount of competition.
The earliest instance of corporate involvement
in politics was over the issue of tariffs.
Tariffs (taxes on imports) and quotas, which
limit the total amount of imports, are important governmental actions that may serve to
protect domestic industries from foreign competition. Bauer et al.'s (1968) classic study of
American business influence in government examined business influence on foreign trade
legislation. Taxing policies as well are outcomes of political action. The controversy over
the oil depletion allowance provides only one
instance in which an industry, through political action, attempted to obtain favorable tax
regulations.

Governmental action also affects the availability of complementary and substitute products. Government action to build roads assists
trucking firms, while airport construction
makes air freight and passenger traffic grow.
In the early days of margarine, the dairy industry was successful in obtaining a regulation

preventing manufacturers from using food coloring to make the margarine look yellow. When
margarine first appeared on the market, a
purchaser received the margarine, typically an
off-white color, and a separate pack of food
coloring, which the purchaser could then mix
in himself. Needless to say, this did not enhance the appeal of margarine; the regulation
was finally dropped.

Through regulation, the government frequently
operates to restrict entry and to permit the
fixing of prices. Regulation, discussed earlier
in this chapter, is yet another example of the
outcome of political intervention on the part
of corporations. But business firms are not
the only organizations active in politics.
Schools, hospitals, cities, universities, and
other social welfare organizations all have
active lobbying efforts and derive the benefits
of political actions. Federal funding going to
public school systems has enabled school teachers to raise their salaries beyond the level
permitted by school bond elections, and some
have commented that the National Education Association may be the most powerful lobby of all
in Washington. Hospitals have acted to obtain
contruction funds, while universities and colleges have lobbied for research funds and
student aid money. Cities, too, have lobbied
for federal cash subsidies. Indeed, it is exceptional to find some organization that does
not attempt to influence political outcomes,
directly or through its membership in an association.

Epstein (1969) has correctly noted that as
long as organizations are affected by political
actions, they will seek to influence those
actions so that they are more favorable. The
power of the state, including the power to tax
and raise revenues, is great. In attempts to
manage their environments, organizations certainly engage in actions to influence the use
of the political process for their own benefits. In each instance the organizations involved will attempt to legitimate the influence

by noting the other groups or social values
served by its claims. Thus, pleas for hospital
construction funds are made in terms of the
requirements for patient care, and tariffs
are justified in terms of protecting domestic
production capabilities, which may be necessary in times of national emergencies. The as-
sertion of claims that what is good for a
particular organization is good for the country
is necessary in the influence process, but is
not necessarily the motivation behind the organizational actions.

INTERNAL INFLUENCE AND EXTERNAL RELATIONSHIPS

Traditionally, organizations have been dominated by those who could most effectively manage internal administrative problems. Skills in
production management, internal control, or
the development of new products tended to be
the most critical skills. As organizational
survival and growth becomes increasingly dependent on the institutional relationships between the organization and its social environment, it is likely that the pattern of organizational influence will change. Political
skills, skills in presentation of the organization and its actions, the ability to manage
institutional relationships with the media and
political organizations, will become increasingly important. Following the theory of strategic contingencies, we could predict now that
in those organizations in which managing institutional relationships is more critical to success, boundary-spanning personnel will have
more power.

The duality of the connection between internal control and the capacity to solve critical organizational problems is a theme we have
pursued throughout this book. The implications
of the present chapter is that one set of critical skills is the ability to negotiate favorable relationships to solve problems of organizational dependence. To the extent that such

problems are particularly critical, these skills at using influence and in developing coordinated and stable patterns of interaction are likely to be more important. What we are suggesting is that the management of the organization's environment may be, or may be becoming, as important an arena of management as the administration of the organization's internal operations. The predicted shift in power is not from those who could rationally administer the organization's internal operations to those who can develop internal flexibility and responsiveness, but to those who can effectively manage the organization's institutional relationships. Given the amount of management of environmental dependence that occurs, the control of interdependence and uncertainy, rather than merely the capacity to react to such contingencies, is a possible objective.

REFERENCES

Allen, Michael Patrick. "The Structure of Interorganizational Elite Cooptation: Interlocking Corporate Directorates." *American Sociological Review 39* (1974): 393–406.

Allport, Floyd H. "A Structuronomic Conception of Behavior: Individual and Collective." *Journal of Abnormal and Social Psychology 64* (1962): 3–30.

Bauer, Raymond A.; de Sola Pool, Ithiel; and Dexter, Lewis Anthony. *American Business and Public Policy*. New York: Atherton Press, 1968.

Bernstein, M. H. *Regulating Business by Independent Commission*. Princeton: Princeton University Press, 1955.

Caves, Richard E. "Uncertainty, Market Structure, and Performance: Galbraith as Conventional Wisdom." In *Industrial Organization and Economic Development*, edited by J. W. Markham and G. F. Papanek, pp. 283–302. Boston: Houghton Mifflin, 1970.

Cyert, Richard M., and March, James G. *A Behavioral Theory of the Firm*. Englewood Cliffs, N.J.: Prentice-Hall, 1963.

Dowling, John, and Pfeffer, Jeffrey. "Organizational Legitimacy: Social Values and Organizational Behavior." *Pacific Sociological Review 18* (1975): 122-36.

Downs, Anthony. *Inside Bureaucracy*. Boston: Little, Brown, 1967.

Elesh, David. "Organization Sets and the Structure for Competition for New Members. *Sociology of Education 46* (1973): 371-95.

Epstein, Edwin M. *The Corporation in American Politics*. Englewood Cliffs, N.J.: Prentice-Hall, 1969.

Farmer, R. N. "The Case for Unregulated Truck Transportation." *Journal of Land Economics 46* (1964): 398-409.

Friedman, M., and Kuznets, S. *Income from Independent Professional Practice*. New York: National Bureau of Economic Research, 1945.

Galbraith, Jay. *Designing Complex Organizations*. Reading, Mass.: Addison-Wesley, 1973.

Galbraith, John K. *The New Industrial State*. Boston: Houghton Mifflin, 1967.

Hannan, Michael T., and Freeman, John H. "The Population Ecology of Organizations." *American Journal of Sociology 82* (1977): 929-64.

Hawley, Amos. *Human Ecology*. New York: Ronald, 1950.

Hirsch, Paul M. "The Political Economy of Industry Profitability: A Case Study of Organizational Effectiveness and the Institutional Environment." *Administrative Science Quarterly 20* (1975): 327-44.

Holen, A. S. "Effects of Professional Licensing Arrangements on Inter-State Labor Mobility and Resource Allocation." *Journal of Political Economy 73* (1965): 492-98.

Jordan, W. A. *Airline Regulation in America: Effects and Imperfections*. Baltimore: Johns Hopkins University Press, 1970.

_____."Producer Protection, Prior Market Structure and the Effects of Government Regulation." *Journal of Law and Economics 15* (1972): 151-76.

Keeler, T. E. "Airline Regulation and Market Performance." *Bell Journal of Economics and Management Science 3* (1972): 399-424.

Kessel, R. A. "Price Discrimination in Medicine." *Journal of Law and Economics 1* (1958): 20-53.

Kiesler, S. *Interpersonal Processes in Groups and Organizations*. Arlington Heights, Ill.: AHM Publishing Corporation, 1978.

Macaulay, S. "Non-Contractual Relations in Business: A Preliminary Study." *American Sociological Review 28* (1963): 55-67.

MacAvoy, Paul W. *The Economic Effects of Regulation*. Cambridge: MIT Press, 1965.

Mead, Walter J. "The Competitive Significance of Joint Ventures." *Antitrust Bulletin 12* (1967): 819-49.

Meyer, Marshall W. *Bureaucratic Structure and Authority*. New York: Harper and Row, 1972.

Olson, M. *The Logic of Collective Action*. Cambridge: Harvard University Press, 1965.

Peltzman, S. "Entry in Commercial Banking." *Journal of Law and Economics 8* (1965): 11-50.

Perrow, Charles. *Organizational Analysis: A Sociological View*. Belmont, California: Wadsworth, 1970.

Pfeffer, Jeffrey. "Size and Composition of Corporate Boards of Directors: The Organization and Its Environment." *Administrative Science Quarterly 17* (1972a): 218-28.

_____. "Merger as a Response to Organizational Interdependence." *Administrative Science Quarterly 17* (1972b): 382-94.

_____. "Size, Composition and Function of Hospital Boards of Directors: A Study of Organization-Environment Linkage." *Administrative Science Quarterly 18* (1973): 349-64.

_____. "Some Evidence on Occupational Licensing and Occupational Incomes." *Social Forces* (1974a): 102-11.

_____. "Administration Regulation and Licensing: Social Problem or Solution?" *Social Problems 21* (1974b): 468-79.

_____. "Cooptation and the Composition of Electric Utility Boards of Directors." *Pacific Sociological Review 17* (1974c): 333-63.

Pfeffer, Jeffrey, and Leblebici, Huseyin. "Executive Recruitment and the Development of Interfirm Organizations." *Administrative Science Quarterly 18* (1973): 449-61.

Pfeffer, Jeffrey, and Nowak, Phillip. "Patterns of Joint Venture Activity: Implications for Antitrust Policy." *Antritrust Bulletin 21* (1976): 315-39.

_____. "Organizational Context and Interorganizational Linkages Among Corporations." Unpublished MS. Berkeley: University of California, School of Business Administration, 1975.

Phillips, Almarin. "A Theory of Interfirm Organization." *Quarterly Journal of Economics 74* (1960): 602-13.

Price, James L. "The Impact of Governing Boards on Organizational Effectiveness and Morale." *Administrative Science Quarterly 8* (1963): 361-78.

Rabinowitz, Larry; Kelley, Harold H.; and Rosenblatt, Robert M. "Effects of Different Types of Interdependence and Response Conditions in the Minimal Social Situation." *Journal of Experimental Social Psychology 2* (1966): 169-97.

Sloss, J. "Regulation of Motor Freight Transportation: A Quantitative Evaluation of Policy." *Bell Journal of Economics and Management Science 1* (1970): 327-66.

Stigler, George J. "The Theory of Economic Regulation." *Bell Journal of Economics and Management Science 2* (1971): 3-21.

_____. "Free Riders and Collective Action: An Appendix to Theories of Economic Regulation." *Bell Journal of Economics and Management Science 5* (1974): 359-65.

Thompson, James D. *Organizations in Action*. New York: McGraw-Hill, 1967.

Volotta, A. *The Impact of Federal Entry Controls on Motor Carrier Operations*. State College, Pa.: Pennsylvania State University, Center for Research of the College of Business Administration, 1967.

Weick, Karl E. *The Social Psychology of Organizing*. Reading, Mass.: Addison-Wesley, 1969.

Williamson, Oliver E. "A Dynamic Theory of Interfirm Behavior." *Quarterly Journal of Economics 79* (1965): 579-607.

Yuchtman, Ephraim, and Seashore, Stanley E. "A System Resource Approach to Organizational Effectiveness." *American Sociological Review 32* (1967): 891-903.

Zald, Mayer N. "Urban Differentiation, Characteristics of Boards of Directors and Organizational Effectiveness." *American Journal of Sociology 73* (1967): 261-72.

7

Change

With the last chapter, we have concluded the central development of a political view of organizational design. We have argued that variables traditionally used to describe structures, such as differentiation, formalization, and centralization, are important as they describe and affect the structure of influence and control within the organization. Further, we have argued that determinants of structure, such as production and information technology, and the organization's environment, affect the power and influence of organizational participants and the resulting structural outcomes reflect this differential power and influence. The theme has been that structure both determines and reflects influence in the organization at a given time, and thus is the outcome of a political process. Such a formulation explicitly recognizes the role of strategic choice, exercised by power holders, in determining organizational design.

Two tasks remain. In this chapter we will consider the topic of changes in organizational structures, again using the perspective developed in this book. In the next chapter, we will attempt to illustrate the utility of this mode of analysis by examining some actual organizational structures in a university. Organizational change is currently a popular topic in the managerial literature. Much of the literature has focused on changing people, rather than structures (see, e.g., French and Bell, 1973; Leavitt, 1965), and most treatments of organizational change, regardless of their focus, adopt a similar managerialist perspective—emphasizing the planning of change to increase the effectiveness of the organization.

THE CONVENTIONAL VIEW OF STRUCTURAL CHANGE

The conventional view of the change of organizational structures proceeds from a series of logically related premises. These same premises form the foundation for much of the writing on organizational change, regardless of whether the author believes the changes should be made by focusing on people, such as through the use of T-groups, or on structures, through organizational redesign.

The first premise is that organizations must be instrumentally effective, or accomplish something of value in order to survive. It is also frequently presumed that efficiency, the production of more output or service per unit of input consumed, is also desirable, but at least instrumental effectiveness, if not efficiency, is required for organizational survival.

Organizational structures describe the division of labor and patterns of coordination. Structural arrangements are important determinants of organizational effectiveness.

Inappropriate structures, defined as not capable of meeting the organization's needs for coordination (Thompson, 1967, ch. 5), information-processing (Galbraith, 1973), or flexibility and adaptation (Burns and Stalker, 1961), produce decreases in organizational performance. Such decreases ultimately threaten the organization's survival.

Therefore, so the argument goes, organizational structures must be designed to serve the needs of effectiveness and efficiency. Organizational structures change when changes in internal interdependencies, the external environment, or information processing requirements make it necessary. In this view, organizational design is an instrumental managerial activity that, like inventory control, production scheduling, or cash management is employed to enhance organizational performance. The most effective design will be adopted.

Many of the authors treating organizational change have belittled earlier operations researchers for their assumption that merely showing someone a better way of decision-making would lead to the smooth and quick adoption of the new technique. These behavioral scientists have correctly pointed out that change involves human factors as well as economic ones, and that it was naive to assume that changes which would increase profitability would be quickly and easily adopted. But a close inspection of the conventional literature on structural change and its underlying premises shows some of the same reasoning. The focus of the argument, but not its essential structure, has changed. Now, instead of dealing with the implementation of inventory control or production scheduling, the authors write of the implementation of System 4 management (Likert, 1961), or Theory Y (McGregor, 1960), or human resources (Miles, 1975). But the premise remains the same—the organizations seeks effectiveness, and all that is required is to demonstrate the appropriate structures and then train people in how to use them.

The neglect of power in this literature on change has been insightfully analyzed by Nord (1974). We can quickly note that the issue of increasing organizational effectiveness begs the all-important question of effectiveness for whom—the owners, the managers, the clients or customers? Organizational criteria for assessment are frequently uncertain, involving ambiguous and contradictory goals and incomplete knowledge about causal relations (Thompson, 1967, ch. 7). Consequently, almost any action can be taken with the justification of increasing the organization's effectiveness. Such a slippery, uncertain standard can scarcely explain observed actions in organizations. While organizational effectiveness may be unclear as a decision criterion, participants in organizations can usually identify how given changes will affect their influence and control. The clear criterion of relative position, we suggest, comes to dominate considerations of change, with organizational effectiveness being used as an arguing point to support those decisions that were already favored.

There are, then, two alternative views of change in organizational structures. The first, and the one that dominates the literature, is that organizational structures are designed and changed to cope with the requirements for technical efficiency and responsiveness to environmental demands. Bennis (1969), for example, has argued that bureaucracy as an organizational form will disappear because it is incapable of coping with the currently experienced environmental change and uncertainty. Coordination and control are necessary for efficient and effective organizational actions to produce desired goods and services. Organizational structure, in other words, is a response to economic requirements, even in the case of those organizations not directly linked to market mechanisms.

The alternative view is that since organizational design is, after all, the determinant of governance and control of the organization,

the allocation of rewards and benefits, and
the serving of certain interests, design and
changes in design are outcomes of political
contests among the various groups and subunits
both inside and outside the organization.
Change in formal structures is better thought
of as a quasirevolution rather than as a process guided by technical or instrumental rationality. It is this latter view that we shall
develop in the remainder of this chapter.

PRESSURES FOR STABILITY

No look at change would be complete unless we
also considered the pressures tending to stabilize organizational structures. The absence
of frequent formal reorganizations shows that
forces tending to promote stability are both
pervasive and powerful in organizations. One
argument for stability is the reduction of the
risk of newness. As Stinchcombe (1965) has
noted with respect to the creation of new organizations, structural rearrangements, to the
extent they are novel, impose costs associated
with their newness. New roles must be learned,
new patterns of interaction must be adopted,
new tasks and relationships must be assumed.
There is a risk associated with the assumption
of new role arrangements—namely, that the
transfer of interactions and activities will
not be smoothly or easily accomplished. If new
roles and patterns of interaction cannot be
quickly acquired, the organization may suffer
decreases in effectiveness and in output. The
ability to assume new roles rapidly is probably related to the previous experience of organizational participants. If new roles and new
structures are frequently required, the organizational members will have experience in such
changes and will be able to assume the new
changes more rapidly. Thus, the liability of
newness is likely to be most important for
those organizations that have stable, infrequently altered roles and structural

arrangements. To the extent that structures have changed frequently in the past, new structural arrangements are more likely to be easily accomplished.

Stability also reduces uncertainty for the organizational members. The present structural arrangements may not be optimal, but at least each participant knows where he stands. Weick (1969) has noted that collective structures of behavior develop spontaneously in interacting sets of persons to reduce the uncertainty experienced by each. Certainly, in a formal organization, with prescribed, stable roles and predictable structures of power and influence, the desire for predictability and stability argues for not making structural readjustments. It has been noted in fields such as economics that persons are willing to trade off higher return for reduced risk. Similarly, in the case of organizational change, persons may be willing to trade the possibility of more control and power in the new arrangement for the certainty of their present positions. Formal structural change has costs—one cost being the possibility of losing influence.

Current structures represent, as we have said before, the outcome of previous bargains. Structural change, therefore, means that negotiations and old conflicts must be reopened in order to establish the new structural arrangements. We can take the issue of curriculum to illustrate our point.

Consider the curriculum in a graduate school of business. Business is a professional school, and comprises several disciplines and subspecialties. However, different schools have come up with different structural arrangements. The structure may officially recognize few or several areas of specialization within the school. The ratification of the legitimacy of a specialization, by its receiving formal recognition in the structure, is important to that field of study and its associated faculty. Moreover, we hypothesize that curriculum design proceeds in the following fashion. Each

structurally recognized area of study receives
one required course in the curriculum, and
those with somewhat more power and influence
receive additional required courses. The curriculum, then, is determined by the structure,
and the structure, in turn, is determined by
the negotiated turf or territories of the various interests within the school. In such a
setting, it is clear that either curriculum re-
vision or structural redesign (and the two are
obviously linked) involves major dislocations.
The legitimacy of areas of study is called into
question, and issues of subunit domain and influence become problematic. It is evident that
the conflict engendered will be severe. The
opening up of such issues throws the allocation
of resources within the department wide open,
and unfreezes long standing commitments concerning relative position and niches.

Stability avoids conflict by not reopening
past negotiated settlements among participants
in the organizational coalition. Precedent, it
is suggested, not only provides computational
and information-processing advantages to the
organization, since decisions do not need to
be made anew; precedent also tends to reduce
conflict within the organization, increasing
the predictability of structural and allocation outcomes and leaving basic subunit domains
and influence positions unchanged. Conflict is
typically avoided in organizations, since members seldom prefer to engage in conflict with
persons with whom they are also interdependent
in an immediate and proximate sense. In the
interest of avoiding conflict, organizational
members will likely tend to favor structural
stability rather than structural change.

DEMANDS FOR CHANGE

Demands for structural change arise from
those who believe that in the unfreezing and
renegotiation that will occur when structures
are reorganized, they will emerge with more

influence and control in the organization. Further, structural change is desired only to the extent that the magnitude and likelihood of achieving the new position within the organization is large enough to overcome the uncertainty and possibility that the participants will emerge with less control than before. This general statement enables us to make some more precise predictions about who in the organization will be interested in structural change, and when such demands are most likely.

It is clear that pressures for change will, almost invariably, arise from outside the dominant coalition. Those presently in control of the organization, unless they believe that by reorganization they can further enhance their control, have absolutely no interest in structural modifications that may threaten their power. Since structural change will typically involve a redistribution of influence, those organizational participants who currently enjoy relatively little influence will be most interested in accomplishing the change. Because pressures for change typically arise outside the dominant coalition, demands for reorganization will typically be perceived as attacks on the fundamental governance structure of the organization. This fact will be important when we consider the strategy of change.

By saying that demands for change typically arise outside the dominant coalition, we do not mean that those in power never initiate structural change. Such change will be undertaken when, as previously noted, it is possible to enhance further the control of those in the dominant coalition over the organization. Change will also be undertaken when it is necessary to forestall demands and pressures from those outside the principal governing group. We would argue, however, that change undertaken to cope with demands before they seriously threaten the governance structure of the organization are still changes taken in response to actual or threatened outside pressures.

Demands for structural change typically
arise, then, from those groups and organizational participants who believe that their interests are not being adequately served, or who
want more of the organization's resources.
Further, since change always brings the possibility that influence can be lost as well as
gained in the reorganization, the proponents
of change are likely to be those who believe
that they have some bases of influence not currently recognized. If a subunit or group per-
ceives that it is obtaining a very small share
of the organization's resources, it will only
attempt to obtain structural change when it
believes that this share of control or resources is less than it deserves considering
its contributions to the organization. March
and Simon (1958) have written of inducements-
contributions balances as determining the allocation of benefits within the organization.
The basic idea is that coalition members make
contributions to the total organizational welfare, and for these contributions, they must
receive inducements at least equal to the
value of the contributions. The organization
itself is a quasimarket, in which the inducements derived from one set of participants become the contributions for other sets. Organizational members are likely to demand structural change when their influence and control
in the organization is less than what they
believe is justified by their importance and
power.

There are several conditions that lead to
demands for organizational redesign. First, the
participants must receive or perceive the possibility of receiving something of importance
from the organization. We all participate in
many organizations, and in some of them our
involvement is minimal: what is received from
and contributed to the particular organization
is not very critical or important to our well-
being. Unless the organization is of central
concern, the participants are not likely to
demand change, as the expenditure of effort

will not be worthwhile. Further, unless they
believe there are resources to be gained, or
that control of the organization is important,
attempts to redesign the organization again
will not be undertaken. By keeping participation in the organization limited, or by convincing participants that control of the organization is not worthwhile, because of the
limited amount of discretion or resources
available, those in power can forestall demands
for structural reorganization.

The second condition necessary before participants will attempt to promote structural
change is that they must perceive the possibility of gaining influence. They must perceive
that they possess sufficient power, perhaps
derived from their ability to deal with critical organizational contingencies, to obtain
more power in the new structure than they
presently have. This suggests that reorganization will be advocated by those with less influence in the present structure than is warranted by their control of critical organizational resources. Reorganization will be opposed by those groups with more control presently than is warranted by their ability to
deal with critical organizational contingencies.

THE CONTEST

The contest over organizational structures
represents a contest for control of the organization. Yet this contest for power is not
unbounded. Constraints on the struggle for
control are imposed by the mutual interdependence of the parties involved. After all, the
essence of organizations is interdependence
among the interacting groups. Because of this
interdependence, there is some need by each
participant for the other participants in the
organization. This mutual need imposes limits
on the extent to which people will go in their
contest for control. Also, unless the

participants contemplate leaving the organization, limits are imposed on the contest for
control by the fact that after the reorganization is accomplished, the members will have to
live and interact with each other.

Because of the mutual interdependence among
organizational participants, norms develop that
provide the rules of the game in the contest
for control. These norms are functional in that
they limit the behavior that will be engaged
in, and thereby prevent the contest for influence from becoming so severe that it threatens
the survival of the organization. Rules of the
game are established to maintain the survival
of the organization. These rules bound the
argument over structural change, providing
limits on both the actions that can be undertaken and on the changes that will be deemed
allowable.

Since rules of the game inevitably limit the
scope of conflict over organizational design,
both in terms of the permissible adaptations
and in terms of the permitted strategies, the
rules themselves usually serve to help maintain the power of those presently in control
of the organization. For this reason, in
especially unstable situations, the rules
themselves may come under attack. Because of
the uncertainty engendered when the norms
governing the contest for control are no
longer in force, an attack on the rules or
norms will generally occur infrequently. In
an athletic event, the particular rules of
the sport may provide some disadvantage to one
team or the other. But the rules do provide
stability and predictability in the contest,
and it is unlikely that the participants will
seek to change the rules themselves, except in
the most unusual circumstances.

There are a variety of strategies available
to participants in the struggle. One is to
form a coalition with other organizational members. Such a coalition means that the control,
once obtained, must be shared, but the gain may
be such, and the necessity such, that

coalition with others not presently in power
may be necessary to have any chance of success.
Our observation, though not derived from any
systematic study, is that in most organizational contests, including those involving
reorganization, the defining axis is between
those in control and those out of power. This
division, between the ins and the outs, frequently transcends differences in training,
information, and socialization. The contest
for influence is the most fundamental of all
issues faced in organizations, and it seems
that this provides the first basis on which
coalitions are formed. For instance, in an
academic department in which control is centralized in the hands of a few administrators
and their cohorts, those out of power will
tend to coalesce, regardless of differences in
disciplinary training or academic orientation.
Of course, once in power, they may, in turn,
fight among themselves, as previously sub-
merged differences now become more salient.
The saying that politics makes strange bedfel-
lows applies, it would seem, to organizational
politics as well.

Legitimacy is important in conflicts over
organizational control. Consequently, strategies for achieving reorganization are more
likely to be successful if endowed with the
aura of legitimacy. One of the most effective
and most frequently used ways of achieving
legitimacy for the reorganization effort is
through the use of an outside consultant. The
role of the consultant as "hit man" is widely
known, but seldom discussed in the literature
on either management or consulting. One problem
of an internal organizational adversary is that
the participants' motives are always open to
question. If a suggestion is made that will
restructure the organization with the result
of increasing the influence of the party making
the suggestion, there is obvious skepticism
concerning the real motive for the recommendation. It is useful to obtain the appearance of
objectivity, and this can be achieved by

bringing in a prestigious, well-paid, and im-
pressive-looking consultant (or consultants).
When the consultant makes the suggestion that
will increase the power of some subunit or individual, or result in the abolition of certain positions, the presumption is that this
is based on objective, organizationally relevant factors. The advice may not be taken, but
it is at least received as being impartial and
unbiased.

Of course, consultants are interested in
earning a living. This means that they are
probably interested not only in the current
assignment, but also in developing a productive and continuing relationship with the firm.
Their interest in future business means that
they are open to suggestions concerning what
they are expected to recommend. The consultant
may be hired at the advice of one of the organizational participants, and may then serve
to legitimate the claims being made by that
organization member. This problem in obtaining
"objective" advice when the advice-giver has
an interest in the future of the relationship
is evident when certified public accountants
respond to client pressure and consulting
firms are hired to do evaluations of various
governmental programs, on the basis of their
willingness to report favorably on those doing
the hiring.

Even if the consultant is not implicitly or
explicitly bought off, the role typically requires reliance on information from within the
organization. Again, control of information
can be used to obtain power, since control of
information virtually dictates the result.

Since legitimacy is important, the use of
rules, or strategies relying on the organization's legal system, are also important. Appeals to outside allies, particularly clients,
may also be used to increase the likelihood
that reorganization will favor the subunit's
interests. Finally, given the interdependence
among organizational participants, there is
the possible recourse to withdrawal, or to

engaging in blocking behavior that will ensure
some level of consideration of subunit interests.

AN EXAMPLE

   The preceding discussion has been rather abstract, speaking of organizational redesign
and its associated causes and consequences in
general terms applicable to a variety of organizational settings. It is useful here to
consider an example of just how such redesign
might actually proceed, and the associated
strategies used to accomplish it.
   Consider the organization diagrammed in
Figure 7.1. This is an industrial company making a technically advanced product. The

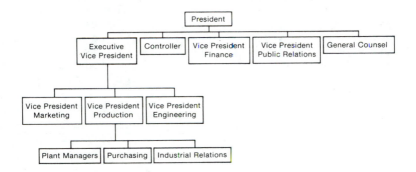

FIGURE 7.1 Organizational structure at time 1.

organization has a division between line functions, under the control of an executive vice-
president, and a series of staff positions,
each reporting directly to the company president. Industrial relations and purchasing report to the vice-president of production, along
with various plant managers. The organization
has been dominated by a production orientation.
Typically, the executive vice-president has
come from production, and the vice-president of
production has been promoted from the ranks of

the plant managers. The president of the
company has most frequently been succeeded by
the executive vice-president. The plants are
dispersed geographically, and the production
work force is largely unionized.

The present structural arrangement is likely
to be favored most by those subunits associated
directly with production—namely the plant
managers and the vice-president of production,
as well as the executive vice-president. Purchasing and industrial relations are likely to
be most unhappy, with marketing also probably
interested in obtaining direct access to the
president. If purchasing and industrial relations are both critical functions, having uncertainty and being important to the organization's success, then the way is set for a reorganization. Problems may occur (or be created) in these two departments. A consultant is
called in, who diagnoses the problem as being
poor communication between these departments
and other high level management. A recommendation is made, and the structure, represented in
Figure 7. 2 is adopted. Throughout this reorganization, purchasing and industrial relations

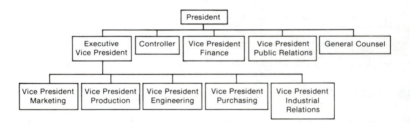

FIGURE 7.2 Organizational structure at time 2.

have worked together, supporting each other's
claims for additional stature in the organization, and arguing for the importance of both
functions. It is also possible that during
the negotiations for restructuring, purchasing
has brought in major outside suppliers, and
industrial relations has used the unions to

argue for the reorganization. This is possible
since the status of the outside organization
is, in part, a function of its counterpart internal subunit. An upgrading in the organizational influence and position of industrial relations, for example, connotes greater importance to the industrial relations function, and
by extension, the unions with which it negoti-
ates. It is always more prestigious to negotiate with a vice-president than with a subunit
director.

Personnel, other than labor negotiations, has
been decentralized throughout the company up
until this time. Now, relying on increasingly
critical and problematic relations with the
union, the vice-president in charge of industrial relations argues for the creation of a
corporation-wide department of personnel and
industrial relations. He uses the federal and
state anti-discrimination laws to argue for the
centralization of control of the hiring process. This claim is buttressed by the corporate
counsel, who is not interested in having the
company exposed unnecessarily to legal risks.
In order to get out of the control of the executive vice-president, industrial relations,
along with the corporate legal counsel, support
marketing's claim to enhanced status. Both
argue for the increasing importance of the organization's external relationships, and recommend that the marketing function be reconsti-
tuted to include the traditional sales, and
also external relations functions. Again a
consultant is called in, presumably with an
external orientation. The consultant argues for
the position of marketing and industrial relations, but also notes the proliferation of
vice-presidents. Thus, the organizationl structure to be found in Figure 7.3 emerges. The
corporate counsel has gained status relative
to the executive vice-president, and personnel
and industrial relations have also assumed more
influence in the organization.

At each stage, the reorganizations described
could be justified by considerations of

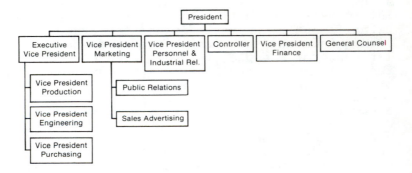

FIGURE 7.3 Organizational structure at time 3.

organizational performance, and improving the
structure to cope with critical organizational
contingencies. That positions of power and
influence were altered, however, may provide
the real clue to what was going on.

LEGITIMATING THE CONTEST FOR GOVERNANCE

Organizational structures are not changed
with public mention of control and power. Organizations, after all, supposedly have objectives, and structural redesigns are always
justified in terms of these objectives. Organizational change is argued in terms of such desirable values as efficiency, responsiveness,
effectiveness, or equity. Organizational members do not argue for structural modifications
on the basis of the favorable consequences for
their own position.

Organizational change is further legitimated
by the norms and values that govern the conduct
of the conflict. Since the scope of the conflict is limited to acceptable behavior, and
since the language of organizational change may
be normatively limited to considerations of objective, organizationally relevant issues, the
mythology develops that change is really being

undertaken for purposes of organizational im-
provement. Such mythology serves to legitimate
the contest for control in the following way.
Participants can now argue for reorganization,
using appropriate terminology, and not risk
being accused of attempting to enhance their
own positions. Discussions take place, with
bounded language and tactics, with respect to
the articulated objectives of efficiency, or
effectiveness, or service. If successful, the
political nature of the process of change may
be hidden from most of the participants. This,
too, is advantageous, since persons are less
likely to be difficult opponents when they imperfectly realize the issues involved.

Parsons (1960), more than most other authors,
has emphasized the importance of legitimacy for
organizations and has noted that goals help the
organization achieve legitimacy (Parsons, 1956).
While Parsons' emphasis was primarily on legitimating the organization in its relevant social
environment, legitimacy, and the use of goals
to accomplish legitimation, are equally important components of action within organizations.
Goals and normatively acceptable values such
as efficiency or effectiveness provide legitimation for organizational actions as perceived
both within and without the organization. This
dual role of legitimation, and the construction
of the meaning of organizational behavior, has
not been extensively examined, unfortunately.

Because of the need to couch the contest for
control in legitimate, acceptable terminology,
the observer confronts difficulty in identifying the causes of the demand for organizational redesign or structural change. Since
structural change may occur for many reasons,
the attribution of causality to a particular
factor, or set of factors, is problematic. Because of the likelihood of multiple causation,
the possibility for attributing structural
change to considerations of efficiency or organizational performance is increased. With the
multiple possible causes, and with the supporting organizational mythology and terminology,

meaning is readily interpreted in terms of a
managerial rather than a political orientation.
Although there is no perfect way to overcome
this problem, the reader should be sensitive
to the possibility that changes said to be attempts to increase organizational effectiveness may be motivated by the demands of participants for greater influence in the organization. Both political and managerial causes
should be considered.

PLANNED CHANGE

The organizational literature emphasizes the
concept of planned change. The implicit notion
is that change is undertaken to accomplish some
intended purposes, such as the facilitation of
interaction to enhance organizational performance. Presumably, the goals of the change are
known and various technologies of change are
applied to produce the intended effects. Similarly, one may assert that changes in organizational structure are planned—they are undertaken to accomplish redesign for some intended
purposes, with intended results.
One's perspective on planning is heavily
conditioned by one's belief in the likelihood
and possibility of rational decision-making in
general. Banfield (1962) has explicitly noted
the connection between normative theories of
planning and the model of rational choice. In
a case study of the Chicago Housing Authority,
Banfield found that planning and rational decision-making were the exception rather than
the rule. Organizational decisions were made
in response to immediate problems, with little
if any consideration of long-range implications. Policy and administration were not sep-
arated. Rather, policy arose implicitly out of
a series of actions taken in response to external pressures and internal organizational
constraints.
We would argue that structural change occurs
in the same way—as a response to pressing

demands created by internal and external
parties interested in the organization. Leeds
(1964) has written insightfully on the absorption of protest in organizations, which is
quite relevant to our discussion of structural
change. She argued that in organizations, protest was frequently handled by integrating the
"nonconforming enclave into the organization
by converting it into a new legitimate subunit" (1964, p. 116). Providing examples from
historical analysis, Leeds noted that the creation of additional subunits and the delegation
of some tasks, but not major responsibility or
control, effectively contained the protest. By
receiving formal status in the organization,
the dissident participants received some stake
in the organization, and thus were not likely
to fight as strongly against the rest of the
organization. The process which Leeds described
we have described earlier in this book as a
form of cooptation. One form of structural
change, then, is adaptation taken to forestall
more severe demands. Structural modifications,
undertaken to provide some increased influence
and stature to various organizational participants, may forestall even greater demands.

Change, made in response to exigencies, can
always be rationalized retrospectively. It
might be suggested that this is how planned
change customarily occurs—first the change,
and then the planning that legitimates and
ratifies the change. Planning may convert de
facto change into formal structural change.
The fact that the meaning of action may be
inferred only retrospectively is a point made
by Weick (1969). Simply put, it means you do
not know what you have done until after you
have done it. Meaning is attributed to, or inferred from the action, but primarily only
after the action has occurred.

Certainly, given the requirements for legitimacy and the maintenance of organizational
myths, it is likely that change, made in response to demands by powerful interest groups, will
and must be rationalized as being consistent

with the goals of enhanced organizational functioning. Seen in this perspective, planning is
itself part of the activity of legitimating organizational change, but is a rationalization
of the changes, not their immediate cause.

SUMMARY

Change in organizational structures is demanded by those organizational participants who
have significant involvement in the organization, who are obtaining fewer resources, and
who have less control than would be justified
considering their contribution of critical resources or their ability to cope with critical
contingencies. Structural reorganization is
resisted by those currently in control, and by
those who have more influence than their importance to the organization might justify. Although the efforts at structural change may be
accompanied by claims that the new structures
will enhance organizational performance, such
claims may be as much a part of the process of
legitimating the contest for control as the
real determinants of action. Conflict over reorganization is bounded by the mutual interdependence of the parties, and this interdependence is reaffirmed by the imposition of
rules of conduct limiting the actions allowed
and the changes permitted.
This political view of organizational change
de-emphasizes the planning process. Planning,
it appears, may be as often a rationalization
for structural modifications as a guide to such
modifications. Further, the notion that changes
are made for effectiveness has been questioned.
Since the critical issue remains governance,
effectiveness begs the question of effectiveness for whom? Structural change can be also
a form of protest absorption, in which disaf-
fected interests are coopted into the the organization. Structural change, then, occurs
when the existing governance structure does
not reflect the real power and influence of

organizational participants. Structure, as both a determinant and reflection of influence, can be out of balance with actual influence and control. There is, however, a pressure for congruence, or the mapping of actual power and influence in the formally designated organizational structure.

REFERENCES

Banfield, Edward C. "Ends and Means in Planning." In *Concepts and Issues in Administrative Behavior*, edited by Sidney Mailick and Edward Van Ness, pp. 70–80. Englewood Cliffs, N.J.: Prentice-Hall, 1962.

Bennis, Warren G. *Organization Development: Its Nature, Origins, and Prospects*. Reading, Mass.: Addison-Wesley, 1969.

Burns, T., and Stalker, G. *The Management of Innovation*. London: Tavistock, 1961.

French, Wendell L., and Bell, Cecil H., Jr. *Organization Development*. Englewood Cliffs, N.J.: Prentice-Hall, 1973.

Galbraith, Jay. *Designing Complex Organizations*. Reading, Mass.: Addison-Wesley, 1973.

Leavitt, Harold J. "Applied Organizational Change in Industry: Structural, Technological and Humanistic Approaches." In *Handbook of Organizations*, edited by James G. March, pp. 1144–70. Chicago: Rand McNally, 1965.

Leeds, Ruth. "The Absorption of Protest: A Working Paper." In *New Perspectives in Organization Research*, edited by W. W. Cooper, H. J. Leavitt, and M. W. Shelly, pp. 115–35. New York: John Wiley, 1964.

Likert, Rensis. *New Patterns of Management*. New York: McGraw-Hill, 1961.

March, James G., and Simon, Herbert A. *Organizations*. New York: John Wiley, 1958.

McGregor, Douglas. *The Human Side of Enterprise*. New York: McGraw-Hill, 1960.

Miles, Raymond E. *Theories of Management: Implications for Organizational Behavior and Development.* New York: McGraw-Hill, 1975.

Nord, Walter R. "The Failure of Current Applied Behavioral Science—A Marxian Perspective." *Journal of Applied Behavioral Science 10* (1974): 557-78.

Parsons, Talcott. "Suggestions for a Sociological Approach to the Theory of Organizations. *Administrative Science Quarterly 1* (1956): 63-85.

_____. *Structure and Process in Modern Societies.* Glencoe, Ill.: Free Press, 1960.

Stinchcombe, Arthur L. "Social Structure and Organizations." In *Handbook of Organizations*, edited by James G. March, pp. 142-93. Chicago: Rand McNally, 1965.

Thompson, James D. *Organizations in Action.* New York: McGraw-Hill, 1967.

Weick, Karl E. *The Social Psychology of Organizing.* Reading, Mass.: Addison-Wesley, 1969.

A Case Study: The Organizational Design of a University

In this chapter, we will use the ideas developed previously to analyze a particular organizational design, that of a typical American university. This will give us the opportunity to illustrate, in specific detail, how the perspective developed can be used both to analyze and to prescribe organizational structures given various preferences and beliefs. We shall conclude this chapter with some arguments to convince the skeptical reader that although the example is a university, the theoretical ideas are equally applicable to other contexts. For now, let us note that Warren Bennis (1964) has argued that the design of the university is good, and in fact is the design of organizations of the future.

THE QUESTION OF GOVERNANCE

Universities have vague, generally stated, nonoperational goals. Take this one, for instance:

> The goals of the University of Arizona are to provide
> the opportunity for the acquisition of comprehensive
> education and usable skills, to serve as a resource
> for the expansion of knowledge through research; and
> to extend the opportunity to improve the quality of
> life by making available the services and resources
> of the University, its faculty and staff, to the
> students of the University and citizens of the State.

This statement, taken from the first page of
the 1973-74 catalogue, supports Parsons' (1956)
contention that statements of goals frequently
serve to legitimate the organization in its environment. Cyert and March (1963) have noted
that vague, nonoperational goal statements are
useful, since they permit all the diverse interests represented in an organization to agree
with them. So, like many other social organizations, universities typically have poorly articulated goals.

The vaguely worded statements of purpose are,
in this instance, probably a function of the
conflicting interests and demands made on the
organization by its various participants. Students are interested in education and training
—undergraduate and professional school students for education and training that will enable them to get a job or that is interesting
or relevant; graduate students are also interested in obtaining a job, but in this instance,
it may require skills in doing research and
publication. Faculty members are interested in
advancing their own careers, which involves
publication and research to provide them with
external visibility, or internal administrative activity to earn political credits inside
of the organization. The administration is interested in retaining its autonomy against both
outside intervention and inside demands, while
the legislature and board of regents, and, occasionally, the state board of education or
educational planning are also interested in
asserting their preferences concerning how the
organization should be run.

The question of control is one of the most critical in the university, and permeates most other issues. Since most of the university budget is spent for wages and salaries, decisions about hiring, promotion, and retention are among the most critical, and one need look no further to see the various interests attempting to assert control. In one Midwestern state recently, in the debate over the university's budget, a measure was introduced by a conservative representative from an agrarian district to strike specifically the line item that would pay the salary of a professor who was known as a liberal and an activist. The university called up all its political strength to have this attempt defeated, which it was. This was not because the administration particularly liked the faculty member in question—he was fired anyway—but because the university wanted to retain discretion over personnel actions. This retention of administrative control (or faculty control) has also been asserted as a justification for vigorously contesting suits in the courts seeking to overturn personnel actions. The university wants intervention neither from the state government nor from the courts.

Conversely, one of the goals of student groups has been to obtain more influence in just these personnel decisions. This has involved developing procedures for evaluating courses and instructors, procedures that by their very existence tend to have some effect. Recall our discussion of organizational information systems in chapter 3. Other activities include lobbying on the campus and at the state legislature to have more emphasis placed on teaching (implicitly, as assessed by students) in personnel actions. Faculty groups are also concerned with preserving professional evaluation essentially by peer review. Intrusions into this process by either students or administrators are resisted. At the University of California, a recommendation that a professor

be given tenure was not forwarded to the
regents. On investigation, it was found that
his file contained news clippings detailing his
involvement (and false arrest) in the infamous
demonstration over People's Park. The faculty
senate attempted to have his name sent forward
again, not because of the overwhelming support
for the specific case, but because of the general principle of governance that was involved.

As in the passage quoted in the first chapter, governance is a central issue in universities. Who controls the decisions and actions
taken is important because of the differences
in preferences and values. If everyone agreed,
it would not matter who made the decision. It
is because of the differences in objectives,
typical of organizational participants, that
control becomes a major focus of attention and
concern.

The Bases of Influence

In the contest for control of the organization, all of the various interests are not
equally endowed with influence or with resources that can be converted into influence.
Following our discussion in chapter 1, there
are at least four bases for influence in the
organization: 1) the possession of or ability
to control critical resources, 2) the control
of or access to information and information
channels, 3) legitimacy of the desired position
or actions, and 4) formal authority, as derived from the formally designated organizational structure and constitution.

Organizations require resources, particularly
money, in order to survive. In a university,
resources are derived from student tuition,
donations from alumni, parents, and friends,
outside grants and contracts, and, in the case
of public universities, appropriations from
the legislature. The resource environment of
universities tends to be relatively concentrated—there is only one state legislature,

and typically only a few sources of outside
grant and contract money that the university
can drawn upon. Students, since their tuition
makes up only a small component of the operating budget, or since they are easily replaced
because of the great demand for admission,
have relatively little power in their ability
to control resources. Alternatively, in those
organizations in which student tuition makes up
a larger proportion of the budget, and in
which students are not as easily replaced because there are not ten applicants for every
position, student control is likely to be
greater.

In order to exercise power, information is
required. This means that access to information
and positioning in the organization's communication structure are important sources of power
in universities as in other organizations. In
order for a department to assert claims to increased resources, or for students to challenge
personnel decisions, the interested groups must
have access to and command of information they
can use to support their case—information
about what is really going on. It is frequently
easier to influence a decision while it is
being made than to undo it once it has occurred. At a minimum, access to information
concerning what is going on is required. The
necessity of having control over information
to exercise power is also illustrated by the
situation of many corporate boards of directors. The directors, with the statutory authority and responsibility of overseeing the management of the enterprise, receive information
either prepared for them by management or by
accountants who are essentially employed by
management. The lack of access to data that
might uncover organizational problems is a
complaint of many directors, made more serious
by their legal liability for malpractice.

It is clear that in the case of universities,
the administrators have the power advantage
with respect to the control of information.
Neither students, faculty, trustees, regents,

nor legislatures have the resources or the independent access to important information systems.

Legitimacy is the third source of influence. Legitimacy, however, is frequently problematic, and therefore is itself subject to competing claims. Legitimacy for some activities and decisions is derived from the organization's stated function. Since we have already noted the ambiguity of typical goal statements, it is easy to see how competing claims for legitimacy could arise. Secondly, legitimacy is derived from appeals to generally accepted social values, or an attempt to identify the group or its interests with such accepted values. In the case of the university, students assert their claims for influence based on the goal of education. Faculty assert their claims for independence and autonomy based on the norms of professionalization, and the accompanying doctrine of peer review. Administrators assert their legitimate right to manage and govern the university, based on their responsibility for the use of various public and private funds.

Finally, influence is derived from position in the hierarchy. Position in the hierarchy, by the way, may affect access to information and access to others with whom to form coalitions, but in this instance, we are speaking of the formal authority to make certain decisions derived from the organization's formal governance system. Certain persons have the formal right to make certain decisions, or more frequently, there is the requirement that they approve certain decisions. Such formal authority rights are established by the formal rules and procedures, which are implicitly accepted by all, though probably known and understood by few.

Similar factors operate to affect the contest for control among subgroups within the major interests identified, such as the various departmental faculty and among the various student subdivisions. For the contest for control

goes on horizontally, among differentiated interests, as well as vertically among organizational strata. It appears that the administrative apparatus, though not controlling a
scarce or critical resource, has the advantages
of information and formal authority, and can
at least assert some claims to control based on
legitimacy. We will next consider the effects
and causes of environment, information and
evaluation systems, and technology on design,
and then examine in more detail the structural
outcomes—the design of a university.

THE EFFECT OF THE ENVIRONMENT ON GOVERNANCE

Unlike some business firms, universities have
managed their competitive relationships poorly.
Excess capacity has developed in higher education, particularly in states such as California
and New York. Revenues are based, at least
partially, on numbers of students served. The
more students, the more future alumni who are
potential contributors. The more students, the
more tuition and the more state support, which
is typically tied to a formula based on the
number of students. Excess capacity, and the
resulting competition among universities, has
had some clearly discernible effects on the
distribution of influence and on organizational
designs.

As already noted, to the extent that universities depend on students for resources, and
to the extent there are fewer students to go
around, the power of students as a group vis-a-
vis universities increases. Although a number
of events make it difficult to isolate completely a single effect, we would argue that
the recent increase in attention to student
demands, demonstrated by teaching ratings and
increasing participation of students in university governance, is in part a result of the
increasing power of students deriving from
their current relative scarcity. When the product or service is in short supply, customer

complaints can be ignored, since there are
always more customers. When competition for
resources increases, however, organizations
will tend to respond more to the demands of
those who have some degree of resource control.

Structurally, the competition for students
makes the operation of boundary-spanning units
linking universities with student populations
more critical. Offices managing relations with
high schools, and even personnel to recruit
students, become more prevalent and more important as a consequence of competition. This is
a simple case of the organization adding subunits to cope with environmental contingencies
that were previously not critical. After all,
recruiting students is not important if there
are many applicants for each position.

INTERDEPENDENCE

Universities have developed some subunits to
cope with the conditions of excess capacity,
but the primary attention has been on managing
relationships with those organizations in control of critical resources. Seeing students
requires visiting a lot of schools, and talking
with a lot of parents. Negotiating with the
state legislature or a few large donors is,
potentially, a much more cost-effective use of
the organization's resources. Organizations,
because they need resources derived from external sources, are constantly being subjected
to influence attempts from these sources. The
dilemma for the university is how to keep the
money flowing without acceding to external demands. This was a theme in Charles Hitch's
farewell address as President of the University of California.

One intrusion of external control comes in
the funding of grants and contracts. The various federal agencies providing funding to the
university expect, in return for the funding,
some influence in the conduct of research activities. Indeed, many of the funding organizations see their role as providing direction and

articulation to research efforts in a given area of study. Of course, the faculty involved is motivated by the desire to increase their prestige and obtain scholarly publications, which may or may not be consistent with the desire of the funding agencies for relevant, applied research. The process by which the funding agency interacts with the university, and by which this conflict over the control of the research effort is resolved, is an interesting one (see, e.g., Salancik and Lamont, 1975). In the case of a large interdisciplinary research project at one university, the RANN division of the National Science Foundation used a very short (six months) grant period to maintain control over the organization; the short grant period meant that the organization was continually writing reports and proposals and justifying itself to the RANN program. Site visits and the proposal-writing process, in which the university is slowly led to propose what the funding agency wants to fund, are other illustrations of the control process in action.

This intrusion of external control is managed in several ways. Of course the simplest is to not attempt to obtain outside grant and contract funds. However, these funds typically provide generous slack resources through overhead budgets, so this strategy is not often pursued. More commonly, the university will establish isolated research units to undertake the grant and contract research. Such differentiated units are relatively buffered from each other and, most importantly, from the disciplinary, academic departments on the campus. Some joint staffing may exist, but this is not necessarily the case. For example, the Center for Advanced Computation at the University of Illinois has some people with joint appointments in the academic departments, but also maintains some full-time, professional employees. By segmenting participation in the research and disciplinary departments, any attempted control on the part of the external

organizations providing funding will almost inevitably be localized in the particular research unit they are funding.

The second intrusion of external control
comes from donors. Particularly large donors,
but frequently smaller donors as well, evaluate
the organization according to how well it is
serving their interests and meeting their demands. It is common folklore that a good
football team increases donations and student
demonstrations decrease them, though no empirical study has been done demonstrating this effect. In this instance, attempts at control are
likely to be relatively episodic and will not
have the coherent theme of, say, the attempts
of funding agencies to redirect research. Consequently, buffering is substantially easier—
accomplished typically through a subunit established to handle alumni affairs. This subunit
will listen patiently to complaints, present
the organization's case, and take the alumni
to carefully selected sites on the campus when
they insist on visiting. Indeed, the visit of
prominent and generous alumni is staged by the
subunit, and is a planned effort to form an
impression. Since alumni typically want some
control over organizational activity, some
universities have established formal mechanisms
by which the opinions of alumni can be made
known. For instance, at the University of
Arizona, large donors are invited to join the
President's Club, which gets to meet with the
President of the university occasionally, and
they are given the feeling of being consulted
about university policy. The alumni typically
have practically no information about what is
happening on campus, and so participation is
easily tolerated since it has no real consequences.

Public universities also face the intrusion
of legislative control. One can pick up the
newspaper in almost any state and note the
contest between the public universities and the
legislature over control of various decisions,
ranging from personnel actions to decisions

concerning teaching loads, class sizes, and curriculum emphases. Once again the organizational response is to establish a subunit to negotiate with this problematic but important external source of funds. In the case of the University of California, there is a vice-president for Governmental Relations assigned the task of lobbying with the legislature. But the universities' primary response has been a claim of professional expertise: educators know best what is good education, and the university, comprised of professionals, should be subject only to peer review, not to direct legislative oversight. Such claims are even implicitly recognized in the appointments of boards of trustees or regents, who are positioned between the legislature and the university. Recently, several states have created state coordinating boards to manage the system of higher education that includes the various universities, state colleges, and junior colleges, adding yet another layer between the political bodies of the state and the university. Needless to say, the claims for professional autonomy are not accepted easily, but again, the legislators have little information about daily operations. At some universities, legislative visits to the campus and communication with legislators are closely monitored and controlled by the administration.

Additional subunits are created to manage the organization's output transactions. Placement offices assist graduating students in finding employment. Since this is a service provided to students, one might again expect that the amount of resources devoted to the placement effort would be related to the influence of students, and various subgroups of students, in the organization. For the most part, however, universities are more concerned with managing their input relationships than with the student output.

In the university, then, we see the operation of many of the factors we had discussed in chapter 5. The organizational response to

environmental interdependence most frequently
involves the creation of specialized, differentiated subunits to cope with each particular
environmental sector, and particularly the
creation of a variety of buffering units to
insulate the organization from the intrusion
of external control (see Thompson, 1967). Research units are isolated from academic departments, particularly when external inter-
ference becomes problematic. Indeed, the differentiation of the organization into subunits,
isolating attempts to gain influence by organizational members, is a common response to both
external and internal influence attempts, and
seems to account for much of the university's
structure, as we shall discuss in more detail
below.

INFORMATION SYSTEMS, EVALUATION AND CONTROL

One of the consequences of the funding problems of universities, caused partially by the
excess capacity and competition referred to
already, and by a general loss of political
support, was a strengthening of the position of
the central administration. We have previously
mentioned research that found that in times of
crisis, the organizational leaders had more
influence. The meaning of any event is derived
through a social process. The fact that universities faced financial difficulties could be
interpreted and acted upon in a variety of
ways. The interpretation most frequently given
to the events was that there was a need for
more and better management, leading to a
strengthening of the position of the central
administration and a general trend toward the
centralization of decision-making in the organization. The response of centralization to
competitive pressure has been noted in industrial firms by Pfeffer and Leblebici (1973).
Thus, the external events were interpreted to
call for more and better management, which led
to the creation of more staff and administra-

tive positions and the development of sophisticated and elaborate management information
systems.

There is little argument that the management
of universities has become professionalized.
Students with graduate degrees in business and
management have gone into staff positions that
have only recently been created. Most organizations now have some institutional research
facility, typically with an advanced information system that permits a variety of analyses
to be undertaken on course enrollment, staffing, and compensation and funding data. Information provides power to those who control
it (Pettigrew, 1973). The development of additional staff and information systems have
enhanced the information available to and pro-
cessed by the highest university administrators, consequently increasing their influence
in the organization.

It is well recognized that through appropriate manipulations one can produce almost any
conclusion one wants from data. But in order
to play this game, one must have access to the
data in the first place. Differential access to
information and control over a large professional staff has led to the increasing centralization and concentration of influence in
the hands of the top administration at the
expense of, particularly, faculty organizations
such as faculty senates.

In an insightful article, Freeman and Hannan
(1975) noted the asymmetry in the growth of
the administrative component in organizations
during periods of growth and decline. Particularly during periods of organization decline
administrative staff may not be cut, and in
fact may be expanded. This author once heard
the phenomenon explained thus: since resources
are becoming increasingly scarce, we need more
professional managerial staff to determine
where and how cuts should be made and how the
limited available resources should be spent.
Although Hannan and Freeman do not discuss
their results in these terms, we would argue

that as Hamblin (1958) observed, a time of
crisis provides the organization's leaders
with the ability and opportunity to centralize
control under the banner of efficiency.

This process is dramatically evident at the
University of California. During the academic
years 1967-68 through 1973-74, the number of
academic positions on the Berkeley campus declined by 6.9%, while the number of general administrative positions increased 20%, the number of senior positions in the Chancellor's
office increased a whopping 144%, and the number of positions in university-wide administration increased 58.9%. The relative changes in
staffing are striking. As enrollments stabi-
lized and faculty positions declined, administrative positions increased. Such a result is
consistent with the argument that crises will
be used by organizational administrators to
centralize control.

CONTROLLING BEHAVIOR THROUGH REPORTING REQUIREMENTS

As we noted in chapter 2, there are two
alternative ways to control an organization.
One involves making most of the decisions at
a single, centralized location, the other, the
use of formal rules and procedures and reporting requirements. It is possible to centralize
some decisions, such as resource allocation,
but many activities in universities are controlled through the use of forms. For, in spite
of what some writers claim about university
governance, most universities have many elements of bureaucracy. We cannot possibly review all of the various forms, reporting requirements, and rules by which behavior is
controlled, but here are a few illustrations.

First, there are course evaluations. These
forms, where required and collected, have an
effect on behavior merely through their administration. Most people obviously behave differently when they know that their behavior
will be assessed. Unfortunately (perhaps

fortunately), most administrators and faculty
do not recognize the course evaluations as the
powerful control devices they are, and hence
they are used to control behavior in a rather
haphazard, unsystematic way. The power of the
forms derives from two sources—first, their
use or possible use in evaluating persons for
promotion and raises, and second, their providing social approval or disapproval to professors. The need for social support is a general one, and professors to some extent require
social approval from their colleagues and students. The course evaluation forms provide such
feedback to professors and tend to influence
the professor's behavior regardless of rank or
status. As Blau (1955) described in his analysis of employment service personnel, professors console each other and provide mutual
social support when they have problems with
their students. In the best operant conditioning fashion, teachers may soon learn to teach
to the forms.

At one university at least, there are also
outside activity reports, on which the professor is to disclose all nonuniversity outside
activity, such as consulting, textbook-writing,
or lecturing. Such reports are not widely used,
at present, but their potential use for in control of behavior, particularly the limitation
of outside activity, is clear.

Finally, there is competition within the
university, as there is across universities,
for students. This competition derives from
the belief of many persons that budgets are
allocated based on students taught, a kind of
enrollment economy (Clark, 1956). This basis
for budget allocation is more imagined than
real, (see Pfeffer and Salancik, 1974), but
nevertheless, the desire to draw enrollments
stimulates competition among departments. Enrollment reports become the basic document of
this competition. Through course evaluations,
and through the operation, even if only imagined, of an enrollment economy, the influence
of students on curricula and personnel actions

has been increased. However, we would argue that the institution of such devices is a function of the increasing power of students largely obtained because of the generalized competition for students among institutions. These procedures merely bring the competition within the organization as well.

Information systems are important components of the governance system in organizations. In the case of universities, we have indicated that external problems have been categorized as problems of efficiency and management, leading to the development of staff and information systems that have acted to increase the centralization of decision making. Rules and forms, such as course evaluations, outside activity reports, and the operation of a quasi-enrollment economy also tend to limit the discretionary actions of individual faculty members. While the bureaucratization of the university has proceeded apace, the mythology of faculty governance is repeated ritualistically, with the outcome that the centralization of power has been accomplished in a subtle, scarcely noticed fashion. The centralization of information and the development of staff permits the control of decisions with the appearance of participation (see, e.g., Mulder and Wilke, 1970).

TECHNOLOGIES

Our point that different technologies are used for different tasks, and consequently that different structural arrangements exist within a single organization is well illustrated in a university. The technologies of the maintenance staff, the food service workers, and clerical staff are all routinized, and hence there is more overt centralization and formalization in these areas of activity. The technology of research and instruction is nonroutine, leading to less control over these activities. One problem in organizations with various structureal requirements is the resentment of those who operate in more tightly controlled structures. Discretion and control, like other phenomena, are assessed through a process of social comparison (Festinger, 1954). The placement of persons who operate in tightly controlled structures with little discretion in proximity to persons who operate with less control is likely to lead to resentment by those with little power. One solution to this problem is the separation of the groups as much as possible both physically and organizationally. This separation between the academic and non-academic components of the university is almost ubiquitous in university structures.

We noted that the issue of routinization was crucial, since persons whose tasks were routinized lost power in the organization. With this in mind, it is interesting to note the attempts to develop computer-based instruction, with programmed text and problem sets administered through computer terminals. The initial articulated objectives of such efforts are to increase learning per unit time and to ensure a uniformity of learning outcomes. The goal of bringing every student to the same level of knowledge for a given topic area assumes the ability to specify and quantify instructional outcomes—that is the first step toward task routinization.

The development of specified learning objectives, and standardized teaching technologies must, it seems, reduce the discretion of the instructor. The loss of influence by performers of instructional tasks is likely to highlight the already visible distinction between teaching and research, as the differences in power between the two functions will grow larger with the progressive routinization of teaching. Indeed, it is reasonable to predict a further structural differentiation that will more completely separate these functions.

STRUCTURE

Figure 8.1 shows the organizational structure of the University of California at Berkeley as

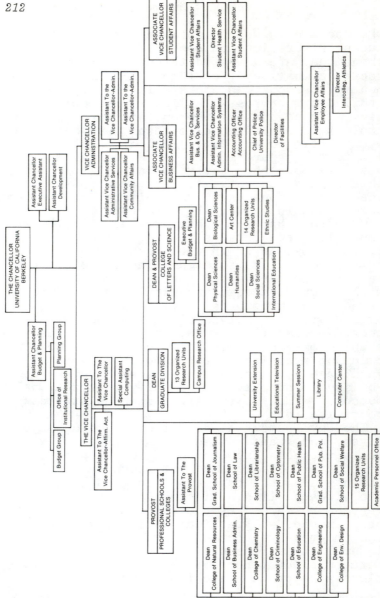

FIGURE 8.1 Campus organization, University of California, Berkeley

of September 1973. A particular organizational chart has been used, but the structural features represented are generally found in most other large universities. We argued in chapter 3 that control was maintained, particularly in organizations staffed with professionals, through the maintenance of elaborate data bases and information systems. Since all persons in the organization espouse norms of rationality, data can be used to win arguments and control the operations of the organization. In this structure, each major higher level administrator has reporting directly to him a person in charge of maintaining data bases. The Dean of the College of Letters and Science has an executive officer for budget and planning, the Provost of Professional Schools has an assistant to the provost accomplishing this function, the Vice-Chancellor has a special assistant for computing, while the Chancellor has an assistant chancellor for budget and planning. Control is maintained, apparently, through the use of the budget, and data on budgeting are collected at each administrative position. Since the work of the organization is done in a variety of locations and is quite varied, direct control over individual activities is impossible. As expected, then, control is exercised through the budget and by the use of information systems and data bases. It is also important to note the tremendous differentiation and elaboration of structure. In an organization with less than two thousand academic staff members, there are more than seventy departments, some of which are not even shown on the chart since they come under the various deans in the College of Letters and Science. As expected, there is some separation of organized research units from the academic departments. Recall that this buffers the intrusion of outside funding and contracting organizations, localizing it to a specific, non-discipline-based unit. Furthermore, there is a fundamental separation between the academic and nonacademic portions of the structure.

Interestingly enough, recently the student affairs functions were shifted to the academic
vice-chancellor:

> Chancellor Albert H. Bowker has announced a reorgani-
> zation aimed at assuring that student services are
> more closely integrated with academic programs and
> academic governance.
>
> "Our primary aim is to relate these student services
> to academic activities, and to interest faculty more
> in their operation. We believe this can be accomp-
> lished through closer integration with the academic
> area, following a pattern generally found on most
> American campuses," Heyman [the Vice-Chancellor] said.
> He noted that Student Affairs services had been
> thoroughly reorganized and their effectiveness and
> funding increased during five years' direction by
> Kerley [Vice-Chancellor, Administration]. (*The Monday
> Paper*, July 17, 1975.)

The movement of student affairs functions to
the academic portion of the organization, and
the increased funding for student services,
both reflect the growing power of students
described previously, which, we have argued,
derives from the changing market for students
in academic institutions facing declining enrollment or at least increased competition for
students.

We would argue that the differentiated structural arrangements represented pictorially in
the chart are an attempt to isolate conflicts
and reduce interdependence among subunits. The
lack of well-defined objectives and the large
number of competing interests represented in
the university require a design which provides
recognition to the various areas of activity.
It is difficult to see how such differentiation could be explained by the relatively small
size of the organization or the complexity of
the environment.

In order to exercise control, it is probably
necessary, other things being equal, to reduce
spans of control. A few years ago, the Provost
positions were created. This relatively new

organizational invention had, we suggest, several effects. First, it reduced the span of
control of the Vice-Chancellor, specifically
placing a provost for professional schools between him and the various professional school
deans, and similarly buffering him from the
various social science, humanities and science
deans. Tall hierarchies have been found experimentally to provide more review of decisions
(Carzo and Yanouzas, 1969), a possible indica-
tion of increased centralization and concentration of decision-making authority. The
second thing accomplished by such a redesign
is to separate more completely the professional
schools from the discipline-based departments.
Enrollments within universities have been
shifting recently, with the tendency being away
from the liberal arts departments to departments specializing in professional (i.e., job-
relevant) training. It is, however, usually the
case that the disciplinary departments were
among the most powerful on the campus, particularly a campus which is noted for its scholar-
ship (see, e.g., Pfeffer and Salancik, 1974).
Under the presumed operation of the quasi-enrollment economy, one would expect a shift of
resources to correspond, at least roughly, to
the shift in enrollments. The imposition of an
additional hierarchical level, we suggest, con-
tains the demand for shifts of such resources
by structurally isolating the departments
gaining enrollments from those losing enrollments. This is a nice piece of redesign, and is
an important lesson to be learned by departments in any organization that have political
power but which face claims on their shares of
the resources. It is important for the subunits to buffer themselves from competition,
just as it is for the total organization.

Control of the organization is maintained
through several mechanisms, including the selective recruitment of presocialized persons
through primarily personal contacts (see
Caplow and McGee, 1958) and through an increasingly centralized process of resource

allocation. When budget resources were more
plentiful, positions were under the control of
the individual departments. If a faculty member retired or quit, the department could use
the salary money released to hire a replacement
or for other purposes. Now, however, at almost
every university positions are under the control of a Vice-Chancellor or Provost. Departments must reargue for vacant positions. Positions and budget can be used, therefore, to
shape departmental and thus individual behaviors. Centralized allocation of critical resources, buttressed by elaborate centralized
data bases, provide powerful control mechanisms.

Figure 8.2 shows the university-wide organization of the University of California. Like
the U.S. President, the office of the president
of the university has added administrative positions and staff over time. And, paralleling
the case of the U.S. President, the likely result has been increased concentration of power
in the higher administrative levels. Notice
in the structure the various boundary-spanning
units, set up to deal with outside organizations and buffer the university from their effects while ensuring their support. There is a
student affairs position, a governmental relations vice-president, a vice-president to
manage relationships with other academic organizations, and a vice president in charge of
agricultural sciences. The special treatment of
this one professional activity conveys some
information about the importance of agricultural interests as a university constituency.

As in the case of campus organization, the
control mechanism is principally the budget and
the data associated with budgeting. Under the
vice-president of the university are several
administrative positions involving planning,
resource management, and budgeting. The relative titles indicate that this side of the
organization may be slightly more important

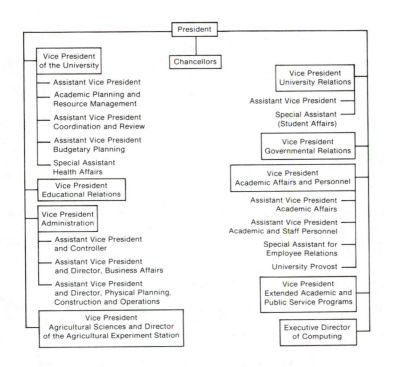

FIGURE 8.2 University Organization

than the other, particularly as direct staff to
assist the president in controlling the organization.

It appears that concerns of efficiency or
effectiveness do not dominate the process of
organizational design. Rather, structure
emerges as a way of dealing with the conflicting interests of various organizational participants and as a way for influential groups
to maintain or increase their influence and
control over organizational actions. Concepts
such as domain, sphere of influence, and a
political model of decision-making (see
Baldridge, 1971) describe the functioning of

the organization. It is evident that many of
our earlier propositions are consistent with
the structure of the university, and with the
changes that have recently been made in the
structure. This brief case description does not
provide an elaborate empirical test of the
framework, but does indicate the usefulness of
this approach to organizational design for
analyzing structures and structural change.

APPLICABILITY OF THE EXAMPLE
TO OTHER ORGANIZATIONS

Bennis may have indeed been right about the
university as a model for other organizations—
not because of its loose, unstructured, adaptive, unbureaucratic design, but because of its
poorly articulated objectives, uncertain technology, and political decision-making. Although we have drawn extensively on the university for our examples, partly because this
is one organization most readers of the book
will be familiar with, we contend that many of
the features of the university are shared by
other organizations.

Take the issue of unclear objectives. One
might say that control and power dominate issues of design in universities because there
are not clear objectives. In business firms,
however, with profit as the overriding goal,
the managerial orientation toward design, with
design seen as instrumental activity, is appropriate. The profit objective, however, is
only one of many objectives pursued in business
firms (see Cyert and March, 1963). It is accepted only to the extent that ownership interests have succeeded in legitimating its
position. After all, why could not customer
satisfaction or employee salary maximization
be equally viable objectives? Profit maximization is based on a model of competitive markets
which does not apply at all in many organizations, such as public and nonprofit agencies,
and applies very imperfectly in large sectors

of the economy that are regulated or where there are very few, large competitors. Even in business firms, Caves (1970) reviewed evidence that risk avoidance, as well as profits, may be sought by managers. It is not the purpose of this book to get into debating various theories of the firm; the debate over what are the "real" goals of the firm continues to the present (e.g., Monsen and Downs, 1965). Rather, we would argue that profit is a goal like efficiency or effectiveness is a goal—it is a legitimate and valued ideal which can be mustered as an arguing point to support one's position. If you want to obtain control over the organization, such control must be legitimated. Legitimation of control is attempted by all authorities in all types of institutions. In some they claim public service, in others, profit, but one must look beyond the public pronouncements and legitimating goal statements, public documents, and mythology to observe the actual basis for action in the organization.

March (1962) some time ago argued that business firms could be conceptualized as coalitions. Examining proxy fights, Wattel (1966) compared them to revolutions. Certainly reading the business press about executive successions, one hears of loyalty and identification with different groups or interests within the organization. Hinings et al. (1974) and Perrow (1970) have written of differences in subunit power. And Perrow (1972) has stressed the importance of analyzing who controls the power of organizations, as opposed to assuming that bureaucracy would either fade away or would automatically serve desirable ends. The focus on influence and governance provides a perspective to complement the focus on effectiveness, profit, and efficiency.

REFERENCES

Baldridge, J. Victor. *Power and Conflict in the University*. New York: John Wiley, 1971.

Bennis, Warren G. "Organizational Development and the
Fate of Bureaucracy." Invited Address, American
Psychological Association, Los Angeles, California,
September 4, 1964.

Blau, Peter. *The Dynamics of Bureaucracy*. Chicago:
University of Chicago Press, 1955.

Caplow, Theodore, and McGee, Reece. *The Academic
Marketplace*. New York: Basic Books, 1958.

Carzo, Rocco, Jr., and Yanouzas, John N. "Effects of
Flat and Tall Organization Structure." *Administrative
Science Quarterly 14* (1969): 178-91.

Caves, Richard E. "Uncertainty, Market Structure and
Performance: Galbraith as Conventional Wisdom." In
Industrial Organization and Economic Development,
edited by J. W. Markham and G. F. Papanek, pp. 283-
302. Boston: Houghton Mifflin, 1970.

Clark, Burton R. "Organizational Adaptation and Pre-
carious Values: A Case Study." *American Sociological
Review 21* (1956): 327-36.

Cyert, Richard M., and March, James G. *A Behavioral
Theory of the Firm*. Englewood Cliffs, N.J.: Prentice-
Hall, 1963.

Festinger, Leon. "A Theory of Social Comparison Processes." *Human Relations 7* (1954): 117-40.

Freeman, John, and Hannan, Michael T. "Growth and
Decline Processes in Organizations." *American Sociological Review 40* (1975): 215-28.

Hamblin, R. L. "Leadership and Crises." *Sociometry 21*
(1958): 322-35.

Hinings, C. R.; Hickson, D. J.; Pennings, J. M.; and
Schneck, R. E. "Structural Conditions of Intraorganizational Power." *Administrative Science Quarterly 19*
(1974): 22-44.

March, James G. "The Business Firm as a Political Coalition." *Journal of Politics 24* (1962): 662-78.

The Monday Paper (Berkeley: University of California),
17 July 1975.

Monsen, R. Joseph, and Downs, Anthony. "A Theory of Large Managerial Firms." *Journal of Political Economy* 73 (1965): 221-36.

Mulder, Mark, and Wilke, Henk. "Participation and Power Equalization." *Organizational Behavior and Human Performance* 5 (1970): 430-48.

Parsons, Talcott. "Suggestions for a Sociological Approach to the Theory of Organizations." *Administrative Science Quarterly* 1 (1956): 63-85.

Perrow. Charles. "Departmental Power and Perspective in Industrial Firms." In *Power in Organizations*, edited by Mayer N. Zald, pp. 59-89. Nashville: Vanderbilt University Press, 1970.

Perrow, Charles. *Complex Organizations: A Critical Essay*. Glenview, Ill.: Scott, Foresman, 1972.

Pettigrew, Andrew M. *The Politics of Organizational Decision-Making*. London: Tavistock, 1973.

Pfeffer, Jeffrey, and Leblebici, Huseyin. "The Effect of Competition on Some Dimensions of Organizational Structure." *Social Forces* 52 (1973): 268-79.

Pfeffer, Jeffrey, and Salancik, Gerald R. "Organizational Decision Making as a Political Process: The Case of a University Budget." *Administrative Science Quarterly* 19 (1974): 135-51.

Salancik, Gerald R., and Lamont, Valarie C. "Conflicts in Societal Research: A Study of One RANN Project Suggests that Benefitting Society May Cost Universities." *Journal of Higher Education* 46 (1975): 161-76.

Thompson, James D. *Organizations in Action.* New York: McGraw-Hill, 1967.

Wattel, Harold L., ed. *Proxy Fights as Managerial Revolutions*. Hempstead, N.Y.: Hofstra University, Yearbook of Business, Series 3, Volume 1, 1966.

Organizational Design as a Political Process

We come to the end of this book. We shall use this chapter to summarize the argument we have developed and to use the theoretical perspective we have advocated to illuminate some issues and events in organizational design.

We began by questioning the customary connection between organizational design and organizational effectiveness. It does not seem plausible that design serves effectiveness, for several reasons. First, the concept itself is used incorrectly and inaccurately much of the time, frequently being confused with the concept of organizational efficiency. More importantly, organizations and their managers have practically no way of systematically assessing effectiveness. Organizations, we have argued, are coalitions of interests. Organizations represent quasimarkets, in which the currency of exchange is power and influence, and the object of the bargaining is the

tremendous energy and power contained in bureaucracies. Since organizations are coalitions, and the different participants have
varying interests and preferences (see, e.g.,
Friedlander and Pickle, 1968), the critical
question becomes not how organizations should
be designed to maximize effectiveness, but
rather, whose preferences and interests are
to be served by the organization. Mintzberg
(1973, p. 95) has identified one of a manager's
basic purposes as ensuring that his organization serves the ends of those who control it.
Unless one defines effectiveness solely in
terms of serving those interests on which the
organization is most dependent (see, e.g.,
Yuchtman and Seashore, 1967), the concept of
effectiveness has little meaning. What is effective for students may be ineffective for
administrators; what is effectiveness as defined by consumers may be ineffectiveness as
defined by stockholders. The assessment of organizations is dependent upon one's preferences
and perspective.

This pluralist view of organizations implies
that there are many groups contending for control, each with a set of preferences and a set
of beliefs about the relationships between actions and consequences, and each with various
resources, including information, legitimacy,
and status, that provide power in this contest.
A continuing conflict is in the interests of
few of the participants. It does no one any
good to have the bureaucracy immobilized by
conflict and the energies of all diverted by
the struggle for control. Consequently, authority and power to control the energy and activities of the organization are divided up, and
this division is partially represented in the
organizational design. The structure reflects
decisions concerning the division of tasks, the
allocation of decision making power, the social
distribution of information, and the control of
the organization. Organizational structures,

then, are the resolution, at a given time, of
the contending claims for control, subject to
the constraint that the structures permit the
organization to survive.

Once in place, the design of the organization not only reflects the outcome of a power
struggle, but influences the future course of
the contest for control. Once in place, structures assume a certain legitimacy by their very
existence. Furthermore, the allocation of differential access to information and differential decision-making authority makes it possible for those in control to take actions to
facilitate their maintenance of power in the
organization. Structures, then, reflect the
contest for power, and in turn affect this contest.

We argued that control of the organization
determined and was determined by the technology
of the organization, the organization's information and evaluation system, and the particular pattern of interdependence with the environment. The organizational technology,
measured by its degree of automation, affected
the extent to which the organization could
adapt its product or service, and consequently,
the extent to which it was dependent on a particular set of input and customer organizations. Furthermore, the degree of automation
and the structure of tasks and work roles determined the amount of control and influence
possessed by organizational participants. The
pattern of interdependence with the environment created various contingencies for the organization. Since power is partly a function
of the ability to deal with organizational
problems, the locus of the contingencies determined the distribution of power in the organization, and hence, the distribution of control
and discretion. The organization's information
system, by providing data to some and not to
others, affected the ability to influence and
control events. The evaluation system determined the criteria to be used in organizational
decision-making.

But since each of these elements determined
the structure of organizational control, each
in turn was the outcome of the distribution of
power and influence as well as a determinant
of that distribution. Technology, information
systems, and even organizational domains, which
determine patterns of environmental interdependence, are chosen, not preordained. We
argued that the choice in each instance was affected by the distribution of influence and the
desire of the organizational participants to
make choices that would enhance their control
over organizational actions. Thus, task routinization provides a way for the power of
some participants to be reduced, while expanded
management information systems may provide additional power to those with access to the system or in control of it.

Because influence affects organizational decisions, the possibility of the institutional-
ization of power exists. Demands of external
groups may be ignored by shifting domains;
claims of internal interests may be avoided by
routinizing their tasks or again by changing
domains to reduce their importance. The picture
of the organization as an adaptive, responsive
entity, proximately affected by the demands of
technology or environment, is probably as misleading as the parallel portrait of the competitive organization in classical economic
theory. Out of the discipline of perfect markets, organizations possess slack, and one
possible use of the slack is to maintain the
position of those in control of the organization. Organizations respond to external demands, but frequently only under extreme
duress. The organization that appears to be
innovative or responsive is so, we would
argue, because such a course of action enhances the influence and resource position of
those in control of the organization's activities.

Organizational change is also the result of
a political process. Change in design occurs
when the distribution of roles, information,

tasks, and power implied by the structure is significantly out of line with the distribution of power implied by the relative control over critical resources possessed by the various organizational participants. Structural modification, we argued, was a response to demands, not something undertaken to improve the organization's efficiency. Of course, it is possible that a powerful interest group demands efficiency, in which case the two outcomes will be empirically indistinguishable. We would argue, however, that the perspective that focuses on redesign as a response to power rather than performance is probably more general and more empirically correct.

The study of organizational design has been dominated by a rationalist perspective, so many of the assertions made in this book have not been subjected to empirical test. Yet, in talking to practicing managers in a variety of organizations, we find that variables such as differentiation, formalization, and the various other scales used in studies of structure partially miss what is going on. We most often hear organizational action, including the design and modification of structures, described in political terms, replete with references to the distribution of power and control, information and status. If the construction and restructuring of a computer department and decisions concerning purchase of equipment can be analyzed using the perspective of power and politics (Pettigrew, 1973), then there seems no reason not to expand this analytical framework to see how well it can account for other aspects of organizations. We next examine some current happenings and theories in organizations, using the framework we have outlined.

THE CASE OF CONSUMER AFFAIRS DEPARTMENTS

Twenty years ago, few if any corporations had a consumer affairs department. Today, there is even an association of consumer affairs

officials, and recently, research has begun on
this interesting organizational adaptation.
Such research is not yet complete, but the general dimensions and issues involved in this organizational change can be outlined.

Corporations, like other organizations, are
coalitions. One interest group in the coalition
is consumers. Since a given consumer interacts
with the organization through a market mechanism, an arm's length transaction, and since
the consumer interacts with the organization
only episodically and typically in transactions involving relatively small amounts, consumers as a group have had little interest in
attempting to enforce their demands on the
organization. Furthermore, because there were
many consumers and relatively few organizations, the organizations had a position of
power with respect to the consumers.

Nonetheless, the central issue is the control
of organizational decisions, in this instance,
decisions concerning product quality, pricing,
and service. Since consumers had little power
and did not attempt to enforce their interests,
they had little control over organizational
actions. The consumer influence was buffered
from the organization. Products were frequently
sold by independent stores or dealers, so the
consumer did not even have personal contact
with the producing organization. Most importantly, consumers, either individually or in a
group, had access neither to information about
organizational policy making nor to the organization's decision-making structure. When
the consumer was dissatisfied, exit (Hirschman,
1970) was about the only possible option.

Through a variety of mechanisms (not important to the argument), consumers have acquired
more power with respect to the companies. Organized in collective associations, which directly attempt to influence the companies and
also indirectly attempt to alter their behavior
through legislative action, consumers have
become a more potent force. Moreover, as the
number of companies, and therefore, alterna-

tives have decreased, the use of the voice rather than the exit option has become more necessary.

The increase in consumer power is reflected by and exercised through the creation of consumer affairs departments. By this structural modification, the company begins to give explicit and formal recognition to the claims of the consumer on the coalition. The consumer affairs department may attempt to influence decisions concerning warranty, advertising, product-pricing and quality, or even product design. Of course, to the extent that the new consumer affairs department is successful in influencing these decisions, the influence of other departments, such as the marketing department, is reduced. Therefore, one would expect resistance to the claims of the consumer affairs department for decision-making authority.

We should also recognize the possibility that the creation of the consumer affairs department may be more a matter of show, in an effort to make the consumers believe that they now have access to and a voice in organizational decisions, without really changing the fundamental structure of influence in the organization. Using Leeds' (1964) framework, the protest is absorbed by creating a new organizational subunit to contain the discontent. This may well be, and probably is, the case. Nevertheless, the example still illustrates the point—organizational structures represent outcomes of a political process, and in turn, affect the distribution of influence within the organization. Consumer affairs departments were set up only when there was a fundamental shift in the balance of influence among organizational participants, and once established, the departments will contend for influence in decisions in which such interests were previously not represented.

We might ask how other conceptions of structure might handle this organizational redesign. One perspective emphasizes the effect of size on differentiation (Blau, 1970). We bet that in a random sample of corporations, size would not account for much if any variance in whether or not the firm had a consumer affairs department. Another perspective emphasizes the dependence of structure on technology. Again, the applicability of this theory to the creation of consumer affairs departments is problematic. Although one might suspect that theories that emphasize the dependence of structure on the environment would be of more use, since these perspectives have typically focused only on environmental uncertainty or turbulence, again the models are of limited use. While turbulence, size, or technology may account for some aspects of design, we would argue that these effects are mediated by the effect of these variables on the distribution of influence within the organization.

We have argued that structures are outcomes of political processes. Consequently, in seeking to explain the existence, size, and influence of consumer affairs departments in organizations, we would stress those factors that might affect the influence of such departments or the need for them to be created. Consumer affairs departments are more likely to be found in more concentrated industries, following Hirschman's (1970) argument that voice is the alternative to exit, and the assumption that consumer affairs departments are established to deal with consumer complaints, not with sales problems. Obviously, consumer affairs departments are more likely to be found in companies that sell directly to consumers than in other manufacturers. Since consumer attention is likely to be a function of the importance of the product or service, we could further predict that consumer affairs departments will be more powerful and more likely to be found in organizations that sell either relatively expensive products, or products that, through their repeated purchase, take a larger proportion of the consumer's dollar.

Power in the organizational structure will be related to the placement of the department in the total organizational design. Influence requires access to information about organizational decisions, actions, and policies at a minimum. Furthermore, it is likely that in order to influence actions, the department must be organizationally close to the decisions in question. Thus, a consumer affairs department put with public relations is less likely to have influence in the organization than one that is part of the marketing or production department.

This example has been chosen to illustrate the points we have made in our discussion of organizational design. While this instance seems to illustrate the relative merit of our theoretical approach, we should note that the creation of consumer affairs departments is a rather common structural modification that is currently occurring. A theory of design should focus on both comparative structures and on structural changes. This is one structural change which is currently quite prominent.

ORGANIZATIONAL DESIGN AS COOPTATION— THE CASE OF PARTICIPATIVE MANAGEMENT

Writing in 1970, Mulder and Wilke noted, "For some time now, and particularly in the last half decade, there has been a noticeable trend in social science literature in favor of participation and power equalization" (1970, p. 430). The enchantment of participation for organizational theorists is evidenced in the writing of Likert (1961, 1967), Bennis (1969), Argyris (1957), and others of the body of thought referred to as Modern Human Resources Management (Nord, 1974). Certainly one critical dimension of organizational design, perhaps the most critical one, is the distribution of decision-making authority. Let us consider, then, what our model of organizational design

and others have to say about the distribution
of decision-making power. At the outset, we
should note that there are two critical issues
in analyzing the distribution of power—first,
how the authority to make decisions is distributed over hierarchical levels in the organization, and second, how influence is distributed over ostensibly coequal organizational
positions and subunits. Others have noted the
relative preoccupation with the first question,
the distribution of power across hierarchical
levels (Perrow, 1970; Hickson et al., 1971). The
phrase *power equalization* is automatically taken to
mean the equalizing of influence across hierarchical levels or vertically (see, e.g., Leavitt,1965).
However, there is certainly no logical reason
why one could not be concerned with the equalization of power across subunits, horizontally.

The argument has been made that participation
provides two benefits that may enhance organizational effectiveness. First, by involving
people in decision-making, they may be more
committed to the decision and more motivated
to carry it out. In the now classic Coch and
French (1948) study, changes in production
methods were introduced into a pajama factory
using one of three different methods with different groups: 1) a group meeting at which the
changes, and reasons for the changes, were
explained; 2) a meeting at which elected representatives from the workers met with management and discussed the changes; and 3) a meeting of all the workers at which the changes
were discussed and decided on by the group as a
whole. The authors reported that the third
method was the most effective way of introduc-
ing change. As described by Kiesler (1978),
commitment, particularly public commitment,
does have effects on behavior, and one effect
is the binding of the person to the action to
which he is publicly committed.

A careful reader might wonder if the experiment described above was really a test of the
effect of various forms of decision-making—
after all, perhaps in the group in which the

workers participated in the decision-making, a different decision outcome occurred. Such was not the case. Group decision-making is occasionally little more than a sham, in which the workers are seduced into thinking they have participated in making a decision, which turns out to be what management wanted to do in the first place. The manipulative side of human relations has slowly been recognized. This, by the way, does not mean that the manipulation is not frequently effective, just that social scientists were stricken by conscience. Fortunately, group decision-making has the second advocated advantage of improving the quality of the decision. In a clear articulation of the differences between the two positions, Miles (1965) called the use of participation to obtain compliance "human relations," while the use of participation to obtain and use the knowledge and skills of the subordinates was termed "human resources." The effects of group problem-solving on performance have been reviewed by Davis (1969), and are treated by Kiesler (1978). Here suffice it to note that, depending on the characteristics of the problem and the group, group problem-solving may be more or less effective than individual problem-solving, and furthermore, some of the advantages of group problem-solving can be achieved using nominal groups (Lorge et al., 1958).

Much of the early research on participation, then, is of little use in a discussion of organizational design. Proceeding from the assumption that participation was a good thing because it increased commitment and motivation and might increase the quality of the decision, a prescriptive, noncontingent orientation to participation dominated the literature. More recently, empirical studies of when participation is likely to be used, and when it is most effective have been conducted. Heller and Yukl (1969) examined decision behavior measured along the dimension of subordinate influence. They found that in comparing three groups of industrial leaders, the higher the leader in

the hierarchy the less centralized was his decision making (1969, p. 234). A group of student leaders tended to be less centralized
than even the highest level industrial leaders. Decision centralization was also found
to differ by functional area (1969, p. 235).
Production and finance were the most centralized, sales and purchasing were intermediate
in centralization, general management and
personnel were the least centralized—the most
likely to involve their subordinates in decision-making. Heller and Yukl also reported
that the tendency to make one's own decision
without explanation was positively correlated
with the time spent in the present position
for all three management levels. Concluding,
Heller and Yukl found that decision-making
was more centralized at lower hierarchical
levels and in business firms compared to student groups; centralization was highest for
production and finance; and centralization
was positively related to the length of time
the manager had spent in his present position.
    It may be plausibly argued that if one ap-
plied an additional scale, measuring the relative power of superior over subordinates, one
would find that it corresponds well to the results concerning decision centralization. Production and finance and the lower hierarchical
levels are likely to have the more routinized
tasks. In view of our discussion of task routinization, it follows that these situations
provide the authorities with relatively more
power, and hence, there is less need to share
decision-making. Similarly, it is likely that
the student leaders studied had fewer formal
mechanisms of control than the managers in
firms, again requiring the leader to give more
control to the subordinates. In those instances, in which Heller and Yukl found inconsistent or weak results, such as the contest
between line and staff and the size of the
span of control, it appears that there is no
relationship between the variables and subordinate influence. In other words, partici-

pative decision-making resulted from the
power of lower level participants, not because of beneficent supervisors.

A similar theme is apparent in the work of
Vroom and Yetton (1973), who conducted the
other major research program on participative
decision-making. These authors concluded that
decision-making, both normatively and descrip-
tively, was related to a set of factors which
essentially assessed: 1) the supervisor's
ability to make the decision; 2) the likelihood
of the subordinates carrying it out, and the
importance of such compliance; and 3) whether
subordinates could be trusted to act in the
organization's (the manager's?) interest. Vroom
and Yetton's data indicated that managers
tended to use the least participative form of
decision-making they could get away with. Although their explanation was in terms of the
time required for participation, an equally
plausible explanation concerns the location of
influence and control.

We can now make some inferences about when
participation as cooptation as opposed to real
power equalization will occur. Cooptation is
likely when the authorities know what they
want but compliance is problematic and important. Real power and participation comes only
when the authorities do not control critical
organizational contingencies, but such control
resides with other positions in the organization.

Cooptation

Gamson (1968, p. 135-42), describing cooptation as a strategy of social control, was one
of the few authors to note the parallel between
cooptation and strategies of participative management. Participation can be used to provide
the illusion of control to many organizational
participants, while maintaining the actual
influence of a few. Because of the possibility
of creating the illusion of decision-making
authority, it is important in analyzing

organizational structures to attend to real
rather than intended or imagined control of
organizational actions.

Mulder and Wilke (1970), in an insightful
experimental study, manipulated both the extent of the subject's participation and the
amount of relative power possessed by the
other (experimenter) in the situation.
The authors found strong support for a direct
effect of expert power, and, more importantly,
found an interaction between expert power and
the subject's participation in creating even
more change in the subject toward the other's
position. Under certain conditions, namely,
when the other had greater expert power, participation not only did not promote real power
equalization, but actually led to even greater
control of the subject. While this was only one
experimental study, the potential applicability
to most organizational situations of participation is clear. While decision-making power may
be apparently provided to many participants,
typically the information-collection and alternative-generation process is done by a very
few. This fact provides the few in control of
the information with expert or information
power relative to the other organizational
members, a situation approximating the experimental conditions created by Mulder and Wilke.

A paper on power and resource allocation in
organizations (Pfeffer, 1977) argued that
participation had several consequences for
coopting organizational participants while not
providing them with actual control. As already
mentioned, while decision-making may be diffused, alternative generation or information
collection is seldom shared. As an example,
consider the hiring process in many academic
departments. Here is a situation which certainly looks like participative decision-making—in
many cases, after all, the issue is put to a
vote by the whole department. But consider the
situation more carefully. The department may
vote on the approval of one, or between two
or three candidates presented. These candidates

have already been selected out of a much larger
pool; moreover, each candidate comes with a
folder of information, which has also been
selected and filtered prior to the decision.
It seems obvious that most of the variance in
who is finally selected is accounted for by
the initial alternative-generation and information-collection process. The final, formal
decision-making meeting is more show than sub-
stance.

A second consequence of participation is that
decision-making responsibility is diffused. If
a single person makes the decision, then organizational members know where to go to ex-
press their preferences and where to focus
their attempts at influence. Indeed, there is
evidence that the behavior of persons in supervisory positions is constrained by the demands
of others in their role set (Pfeffer and
Salancik, 1975). But if decision-making is
ostensibly diffused over many members, it becomes more difficult for persons interested in
the decision to know where and how to exert
influence. The apparent diffusion of decision-
making, then, actually acts to insulate the
decision-making process from influence.

Finally, by providing persons with some
organizational legitimacy and some feeling of
participation, one may divert their attention
from their initial focus to one of maintaining
their limited position within the organization.
We may consider the case of either students or
feminists at universities as an illustration of
the successful use of such a strategy. At a
large university in the Midwest, the situation
of women staff members was poor; there was
apparent discrimination in pay, promotion, and
hiring practices (see, e.g., Loeb and Ferber,
1971); and the university had settled a large
wage case brought by members of the custodial
staff. Female graduate students were also typically poorly treated, especially in traditionally male fields. The university's response
to increasing pressure from women was to establish a Committee on the Status of Women. The

committee was given a research assistant, stationery, official university recognition, and occasional meetings with high-level administrators. The bureaucratization of the protest was striking. The committee was populated by the more vocal and powerful feminists, but once on the committee, just as Leeds (1964) suggested, many of them became more interested in the organization than in the original goals. The use of the research assistant, maintenance of official status and access to administrators, and the following of bureaucratic forms came to dominate attention. There was, of course, a consequent reduction in the level of effort expended to accomplish the reforms that were the original focus of attention.

The war on poverty provides yet another illustration of participation used as cooptation. Some have maintained (see, e.g., Marshall, 1971) that the only goal of the war on poverty was to cool off the urban protests by absorbing, in a variety of ways, militant urban political leaders. In this instance, two forms of cooptation were used. First, activists were recruited for government jobs in the poverty agencies. Needless to say, once they had $18,000—$20,00 a year jobs, the revolutionary ardor of the leaders cooled. Second, various advisory boards were established to provide citizen input into the operation of the various community agencies. As in the case of the women in universities, membership on the committees and the operation of the committees became ends in themselves, and the original aims and claims of the organizational members became diffused.

The extent to which change was accomplished, and the extent to which actual cooptation occurred, are empirical issues and will vary with the situation being examined. Nevertheless, the modality of the organizational structural response to pressure is clear—the creation of a subunit to provide limited access and a feeling of participation in organizational decisions. Again, we can see that

structures adapt to the realities of power,
but in a way to maintain as much of the power
of the original influential people as possible.

STRUCTURES AS COMPROMISE

Besides participation in decision-making,
another major theme of research in organizational structure has been differentiation in
organizations (see, e.g., Blau, 1970; Blau and
Schoenherr, 1971; Meyer, 1972). Differentiation is related to the division of labor, and
has most often been measured by the number of
subunits (departments) and by the number of
levels in the organization's hierarchy. The
concept refers to the extent to which the
tasks in the organization are divided into
small, specialized components, or the extent
to which there is less specialization and
differentiation of function in the organization. Most of the research has pursued the
theme of the effect of size on differentiation
(see, e.g., Meyer, 1972; Blau, 1970).

But there is another possible perspective
on differentiation, suggested by Thompson
(1967). We have argued that organizations are
coalitions, comprising at any time persons and
groups with diverse preferences and interests.
Clearly in such a case conflict over decisions
concerning organizational actions is almost
inevitable. But we have also noted that per-
petual conflict will only tend to immobilize
the organization, serving the interests of no
one. After all, the various groups want to control the organization's energy, not dissipate
it. Cyert and March (1963) have suggested that
one way conflict is avoided is by attending to
the various preferences and goals sequentially.
While not denying that this is a used and useful method of conflict management, we argue
that another way that conflict among organizational participants is managed is through differentiation and structural elaboration.

Simply put, instead of attempting to resolve the conflicts, which is probably impossible, and in addition to attending to preferences sequentially, organizational participants are given, through structural differentiation, unique domains in which they can control activity and obtain satisfaction of their interests. If, for instance, there is a conflict between research and teaching in a university, one structural solution is to differentiate the organization, establishing subunits for research and subunits in which instruction is the primary activity. Such differentiation enables the various participants to act in isolation from those with whom they might be in conflict, while the total organization retains the membership and actions of all. This notion is quite similar to the theme pursued by Lawrence and Lorsch (1967), who noted that organizations require differentiation in order to maintain different time perspectives and different goals. However, rather than focusing on differentiation solely as a function of the organization's environment, we would argue that differentiation is a consequence of the diversity and incompatibility of participants in the coalition.

It seems that carving up organizations and giving out pieces of turf—domains—to various subunits or interest groups is a common response to organizational conflicts. Such a strategy, of course, is probably easier when the organization is large or has sufficient resources to permit many different activities to go on, which may account for the observed relationship between differentiation and size. Organizational designs, therefore, are the result of compromises. Rather than deciding between activities, preferences, and definitions of reality, the organization may be structured so that each interest has some domain of activity. In the differentiated structure, conflict is reduced by uncoupling the interdependence among subunits.

This line of argument suggests a corollary
hypothesis to Thompson's argument (1967, p.
29) concerning the number of political positions in the organization. The larger and more
diverse the coalition that constitutes the organization, the more differentiated the organization is likely to be, permitting each of
the diverse interests to operate with a minimum amount of interdependence and thus conflict with others in the organization. Differentiation, therefore, not only causes differences in goals and values through subgroup
identification, but it is, occasionally, also
a response to the diverse interests represented within organizations.

The compromise represented by the organizational design is managed through the organization's hierarchy. Thompson (1967) argued that
one of the functions of hierarchy was to resolve conflicts which could not be solved at
lower levels, and noted that the hierarchy of
the organization included increasingly large
units of interdependence. Lawrence and Lorsch
(1967) detailed additional integrating devices besides the formal hierarchy, including
special integrator roles and committees. However, the modal response is probably the management of the compromise through the hierarchy.

Certainly, as Cyert and March (1963) argued,
the conflict implicit in the coalitional view
of organizations is imperfectly resolved. One
manifestation of this is likely to be structures which appear to have inconsistencies in
them. Such inconsistencies may involve duplicate activities or functions, or subunits apparently working at cross-purposes. A rationalist perspective would argue that such
inconsistencies reduce organizational performance and should be eliminated. Such a view,
however, neglects the possibility that these
structural inconsistencies may be a reasonable
response to the conflicting demands and interests of organizational participants.

CONCLUSION

The phrase *organizational design*, the title of
this book, implies an active, managerial effort to structure organizations to achieve some
purpose. In a sense, then, there appears to be
a contradiction between the title, which
stresses the efficacy of rational managerial
action, and the book itself, which has emphasized the political nature of structures, and
has described organizational design outcomes as
both causes and consequences of underlying
political forces operating in and between organizations. Such a contradiction is both
functional and only partially true.

People tend to be either-or thinkers—either
this must be true, or that must be true.
Choices between theories of reality, including
the reality of organizational behavior, are
also frequently put into an either-or framework. Alternatively, a dialectic approach
posits the possibility that both x and not x
may be true, and traces the consequences of
each. Such a process presumably enhances understanding and insight. Since the conventional
wisdom does not, it seems, account for a lot
of the variance, we have offered this alternative perspective as an additional way of getting insight into organizational design. It
may not be either-or, but both.

Furthermore, the contradiction may be only
partially true. It is not necessarily a contradiction to note that organizational structures
emerge as a consequence of the interplay of
political forces, and at the same time recognize that managers may have some discretion
in using and manipulating these forces. Indeed, we would argue that it is only through
being able to understand and recognize the
various factors that constrain managerial action that a manager can use the discretion and
latitude he does possess. A similar point has
been made by Pettigrew who wrote:

An accurate perception of the power distribution in
the social arena in which he lives is therefore a
necessary prerequisite for the man seeking powerful
support for his demands. . . . Bailey (1969, p. 108)
makes this point well: "Knowledge is power. The man
who correctly understands how a particular structure
works can prevent it from working or make it work
differently with much less effort than a man who does
not know these things. This may seem obvious yet actions are often taken without previous analysis and
out of ignorance." (1973, p. 240)

We have tried to serve a dual purpose—to explain why structures are the way they are and
also to describe strategies and tactics that
are used in organizational design. The two perspectives are at once both compatible and contradictory.

REFERENCES

Argyris, Chris. *Personality and Organization.* New York:
Harper, 1957.

Bailey, F. G. *Strategems and Spoils: A Social Anthro-
pology of Politics.* Oxford: Blackwell, 1969.

Bennis, Warren G. *Organization Development: Its Nature,
Origins, and Prospects.* Reading, Mass.: Addison-
Wesley, 1969.

Blau, Peter M. "A Formal Theory of Differentiation in
Organizations." *American Sociological Review 35* (1970):
201-18.

Blau, Peter M., and Schoenherr, Richard A. *The Structure
of Organizations.* New York: Basic Books, 1971.

Coch, Lester, and French, John R. P., Jr. "Overcoming
Resistance to Change." *Human Relations 1* (1948): 512-
32.

Cyert, Richard M., and March, James G. *A Behavioral
Theory of the Firm.* Englewood Cliffs, N.J.: Prentice-
Hall, 1963.

Davis, James H. *Group Performance*. Reading, Mass.: Addison-Wesley, 1969.

Friedlander, F., and Pickle, H. "Components of Effectiveness in Small Organizations." *Administrative Science Quarterly 13* (1968): 289-304.

Gamson, William A. *Power and Discontent*. Homewood, Ill.: Dorsey Press, 1968.

Heller, Frank, and Yukl, Gary. "Participation, Managerial Decision-Making, and Situational Variables." *Organizational Behavior and Human Performance 4* (1969): 227-41.

Hickson, D. J.; Hinings, C. R.; Lee, C. A.; Schneck, R. E.; and Pennings, J. M. "A Strategic Contingencies' Theory of Intraorganizational Power." *Administrative Science Quarterly 16* (1971): 216-29.

Hirschman, Albert O. *Exit, Voice, and Loyalty*. Cambridge, Mass.: Harvard University Press, 1970.

Kiesler, S. *Interpersonal Processes in Groups and Organizations*. Arlington Heights, Ill.: AHM Publishing Corporation, 1978.

Lawrence, Paul, and Lorsch, Jay. *Organization and Environment*. Boston: Division of Research, Harvard Business School, 1967.

Leavitt, Harold J. "Applied Organizational Change in Industry: Structural, Technological and Humanistic Approaches." In *Handbook of Organizations*, edited by James G. March, pp. 1144-70. Chicago: Rand McNally, 1965.

Leeds, Ruth. "The Absorption of Protest: A Working Paper." In *New Perspectives in Organization Research,* edited by W. W. Cooper, H. J. Leavitt, and M. W. Shelly, pp. 115-35. New York: John Wiley, 1964.

Likert, Rensis. *New Patterns of Management*. New York: McGraw-Hill, 1961.

_____. *The Human Organization*. New York: McGraw-Hill, 1967.

Loeb, Jane, and Ferber, Marianne. "Sex as Predictive of

Salary and Status on a University Faculty." *Journal of Educational Measurement* 8 (1971): 235-44.

Lorge, I.; Fox, D.; Davitz, J.; and Brenner, M. "A Survey of Studies Contrasting the Quality of Group Performance and Individual Performance, 1920-1957." *Psychological Bulletin* 55 (1958): 337-72.

Marshall, Dale Rogers. *The Politics of Participation in Poverty*. Berkeley: University of California Press, 1971.

Meyer, Marshall W. *Bureaucratic Structure and Authority*. New York: Harper and Row, 1972.

Miles, Raymond E. "Human Relations or Human Resources?" *Harvard Business Review* 43 (July-August 1965): 148-63.

Mintzberg, Henry. *The Nature of Managerial Work*. New York: Harper and Row, 1973.

Mulder, Mark, and Wilke, Henk. "Participation and Power Equalization." *Organizational Behavior and Human Performance* 5 (1970): 430-48.

Nord, Walter R. "The Failure of Current Applied Behavioral Science—A Marxian Perspective." *Journal of Applied Behavioral Science* 10 (1974): 557-78.

Perrow, Charles. "Departmental Power and Perspective in Industrial Firms." In *Power in Organizations*, edited by Mayer N. Zald, pp. 59-89. Nashville: Vanderbilt University Press, 1970.

Pettigrew, Andrew M. *The Politics of Organizational Decision-Making*. London: Tavistock, 1973.

Pfeffer, Jeffrey. "Power and Resource Allocation in Organizations." In *New Directions in Organizational Behavior*, edited by B. M. Straw and G. R. Salancik, pp. 235-65. Chicago: St. Clair Press, 1977.

Pfeffer, Jeffrey, and Salancik, Gerald R. "Determinants of Supervisory Behavior: A Role Set Analysis." *Human Relations* 28 (1975): 139-54.

Thompson, James. *Organizations in Action*. New York: McGraw-Hill, 1967.

Vroom, Victor H., and Yetton, Philip W. *Leadership and Decision-Making*. Pittsburgh: University of Pittsburgh Press, 1973.

Yuchtman, E., and Seashore, S. E. "A System Resource Approach to Organizational Effectiveness." *American Sociological Review 32* (1967): 891–903.

Name Index

Subject Index